Freddie North

CONVENTIONAL BIDDING EXPLAINED

B. T. Batsford Ltd, *London*

First published 1994

© Freddie North 1994

0 7134 7643 5

Typeset by Apsbridge Services Ltd, Nottingham.
Printed by Redwood Books, Trowbridge, Wiltshire
for the publishers,
B. T. Batsford Ltd, 4 Fitzhardinge Street,
London W1H 0AH

A BATSFORD BRIDGE BOOK
Series Editor: Tony Sowter

CONTENTS

FOREWORD

It is now over twenty years ago that I gave up any thoughts of a nine-to-five existence and committed my life to bridge. At that time I became a regular in London bridge clubs, trying to supplement my income at the rubber-bridge tables. It was then that I first met Freddie North. He was one of the better known players around, but did not display the arrogance of some of his peers. He always had time and a word of advice for even the weakest of players. The plain commonsense of what he told people I am sure stayed in their minds for a very long time.

It is no surprise to me that Freddie has concentrated more on teaching and writing about the game in more recent years. The clarity of his thought has made the game appear easier for thousands of bridge players. This book is the long-overdue distillation of his bridge wisdom. It is a look at the tools used in modern-day competition, and an analysis of their worth. Only the treatments that have proved themselves winners over many years of use and, from time to time I am sorry to say, misuse are included. The more fanciful flights of imagination are left alone. The reader is invited to look at a problem area, investigate a solution and then look at the solution in operation where it matters – at the bridge table. There is no-one who will not benefit from reading this bridge book with its pages of practical and sensible advice. Go forth and enjoy.

Zia Mahmood
April 1994

ACKNOWLEDGEMENTS

I am especially grateful to *Bridge Magazine* for publishing a whole series of articles under the banner 'What's it all about?'. This has given me the inspiration to write this book, because so many players have told me how they learned and enjoyed reading about conventions which were not clear to them before.

Some of the articles are reproduced with little or no change. Others have been updated with extra material added, while a few are completely new.

My thanks to Glyn Liggins for his efforts to try and eradicate my own shortcomings and generally keep me on the straight and narrow!

Freddie North
July 1994

INTRODUCTION

In my experience of teaching and writing about bridge, I have become increasingly aware of a certain need amongst the improving and aspiring players. They would like to learn in a simple way. They would like to know the facts, but perhaps not too many. They would like to know something about the popular conventions, and how best to use them.

Obviously it would not be possible to cover the whole gamut of bridge expertise, or even all the essentials, in one book, and, indeed, this is not my intention. What I have endeavoured to do is to introduce many of the more popular conventions, and useful tactics in defence so that readers can equip themselves to face the world and do battle on more equitable terms than would otherwise be the case.

Many of the finest players in the world have found it unnecessary to use a multiplicity of conventions. Names like Gabriel Chagas and Marcelo Branco from Brazil, the four French world champions Paul Chemla, Michel Perron, Alain Levy and Hervé Mouiel are a few names that spring readily to mind, not to mention former world champions like Bobby Slavenburg and Hans Kreyns from the mid-sixties. But to look at the modern-day convention cards of some players you would be excused for mildly raising your eyebrows at the conglomeration of gadgetry. Having said that, there is no doubt that by attaching some useful conventions to your repertoire and by understanding the everyday language of bridge – the encouraging sequences, the sign-offs and the nuances – your game will surely improve immeasurably.

I have given a Star Rating to each convention. Five stars is a very strong recommendation that you study the subject well. One star suggests that you can probably live without it, or at least postpone study until a later date, while the in-between stars reflect the importance of the subject as I see it.

Ah well, now we know what this book is all about, our role together is to sort out what you need, what you enjoy and what you can take on board. Let simplicity and understanding be the key words. We'll walk first, run later and, maybe much later, think about sprinting.

Freddie North
July 1994

1

HAND EVALUATION

When first you pick up your hand, you need easily memorable rules of thumb to help you make a working assessment of the hand's potential. Your assessment may change as the auction develops, but initially you need a broadly accurate estimate of your strength. To achieve this you need a good understanding of the Milton Work Point-Count.

The Milton Work Point-Count

Star Rating: ✱✱✱✱✱

While countries around the world may have different mother tongues and different currencies, bridge is fortunate to enjoy a common language that everybody speaks, a common currency that everyone understands. It's called the Point-Count, publicised by the American Milton Work.

$$
\begin{array}{rcl}
\text{Ace} & = & 4 \\
\text{King} & = & 3 \\
\text{Queen} & = & 2 \\
\text{Jack} & = & 1
\end{array}
$$

Although there are a number of anomalies, this simple formula proved so popular that its universal adoption was virtually guaranteed, and yet, paradoxically, it is because of this simplistic valuation that an inherent danger lurks. The danger is that, while experts know how to adjust the points with pluses or minuses as the auction develops, or even before it starts, many less experienced players rely almost religiously on the basic point-count, just as though it were some omnipotent dogma that must never be questioned or altered.

Generally speaking, the point-count for no trump contracts on balanced hands works out fairly well. However, sometimes we have to adopt a practical approach. Suppose you play a 12-14 point no trump opening bid, with a 15-16 point rebid, and hold the following hands:

(a) ♠ KQ3
     ♡ Q65
     ◇ KQ4
     ♣ K763

(b) ♠ KQ10
     ♡ A9
     ◇ 1098
     ♣ AJ1096

The point count fanatic, with his 15 points on (a), would no doubt open one club and show his 'extra strength' by rebidding 1NT. On (b), as he has only 14 points, he would probably open 1NT, feeling confident that he was playing according to the system (12-14 points = a 1NT opening bid).

In fact, the very opposite approach is much more realistic. Hand (a), with its poor shape and complete lack of intermediate cards like tens and nines, should be downgraded to a 1NT opening bid, while hand (b), with its exceptional intermediates and five-card suit, should be upgraded to a 1NT rebid. It is worth every penny of the 15-16 points that the rebid will advertise.

So we've seen with our first example how intermediates (stuffing or undergrowth as it is sometimes called) or lack of them can influence our opening bid. What about our response to a 1NT opening (12-14)? Most text books tell you to raise 1NT to 2NT on 11-12 points. Sound enough in basic form, but dangerous if the point count addict sticks slavishly to his points. Partner opens 1NT (12-14). You hold:

(a) ♠ QJ4
     ♡ K63
     ◇ K43
     ♣ Q742

(b) ♠ A108
     ♡ K9
     ◇ A1083
     ♣ 10853

(c) ♠ A108
     ♡ K9
     ◇ AJ1083
     ♣ 1097

(d) ♠ 83
     ♡ A75
     ◇ Q104
     ♣ AJ10986

What would you bid in each case after your partner opens 1NT and the next hand passes?

(a) I remember taking part in a seminar with Jeremy Flint when we put up a hand similar to this and posed the same question. The overwhelming answer was 2NT. 'Eleven points are eleven points, aren't they?' seemed to be the mood of the class. It took us longer on this question than any other to persuade our audience that 'Pass' was the right bid. With such an empty 11 points, and the worst possible shape, there is very little merit in suggesting game. It is much better to downgrade the hand by a point when, of course, you have a comfortable pass.

(b) Now you are on firm ground for a raise to 2NT. The intermediates are excellent and the two four card suits offer additional scope.

(c) We have 12 HCPs (high-card points), so should we raise to 2NT? No, we should not! This hand needs upgrading to a good 13+ and we should bid a confident 3NT.

(d) This time we have only 11 HCPs – so? Again, a case for upgrading. The six card suit with good intermediates does not lend itself to planting the decision in partner's lap. Best to bid 3NT and hope it keeps fine. It will, most of the time.

Your opening bid of 2NT is based on 20-22 points. What would you open on the following hands?

(a) ♠ Q53	(b) ♠ A106	(c) ♠ A106
♡ KQJ6	♡ A10983	♡ AK1098
◇ AKQ	◇ AJ	◇ AJ
♣ K53	♣ AQ10	♣ AQ10

Let us see if the message is beginning to strike a chord

(a) Although we have the point-count for a 2NT opening, there is much to be said for starting with 1♡ (just assume you have 19 points). Lacking any tenace positions, and with poor shape, it wouldn't be a tragedy if partner passed. However, if partner does respond 1NT maybe he holds some tenaces and 3NT will play better from his side of the table.

(b) This time we have 19 HCPs, but what a 19! With all four aces you should always add one extra point (the ace is slightly undervalued at four points). That brings us to 20 points, plus a five card suit and good tenaces. It all adds up to a sound 2NT opening.

(c) This time we have 22 HCPs, so do we have a maximum 2NT opening? No, we are too good. The four aces (plus one point) and a fine five card suit makes us worth a 2♣ opening with a rebid of 2NT over a 2◇ response. Advertising 23-24 points is more accurate valuation than announcing 20-22.

There is another situation where it is necessary to consider the suitability of the points, rather than their number. Most players know how to apply distributional aids but are less proficient when it comes to upgrading or downgrading their high cards. When the high cards are together in the long suit the hand becomes attractive to play.

♠ AQ975
♡ A10843
◊ 65
♣ 4

This hand may contain only 10 HCPs but all experienced players will surely open it with one spade. The honour cards are well placed with the length, and justice will never be done to it if the holder passes.

By contrast, consider the same 10 points in this setting:

♠ 97543
♡ A8543
◊ A10
♣ Q

Now, with the rearrangement of the top cards, the hand becomes unattractive to open. Best to pass and listen.

When the honour cards are in the short suits, defence is more likely to appeal than offence.

(a) ♠ AJ	(b) ♠ AJ83
♡ J873	♡ J7
◊ AQ	◊ 43
♣ J8754	♣ AQJ85

Both hands contain the same number of points, but whereas (b) is a clear-cut opening of one club, with an easy rebid of one spade, (a), with the honour cards in the short suits, is a hand full of misgivings – unless defending at a conveniently high level when it would probably be superior to (b). No doubt we must open hand (a) and, despite the slightly off-beat shape, my strong preference is for 1NT – often a good opening when the long suits are weak and the short suits contain tenaces and honours that need protecting.

Although the next two hands also contain the same number of points, (a) is likely to be superior to (b).

(a) ♠ AK864	(b) ♠ AK864
♡ KQ7	♡ KQ
◊ QJ4	◊ Q74
♣ 75	♣ J75

So we can say this; king-queen doubletons, singleton honours and unsupported honours, like Qxx or Jxx, should be regarded as minus values
unless they are known to blend with partner's suit. On the other hand, tens
added to honour cards as in Q10x, QJ10, KQ10, A10x, J10x, may make a
significant difference to the combined values and, therefore, must be
looked on favourably.

With only the opposition vulnerable, your right-hand opponent bids one
heart. You hold one of the following hands:

	(a) ♠ Q7	(b) ♠ 53
	♡ Q64	♡ 64
	◇ AJ864	◇ AKJ1086
	♣ KJ6	♣ 864

Well, are you going to intervene? If you do, would you prefer hand (a) or
hand (b)?

I don't see this as a contest, and perhaps you feel the same, but the point-
count addict will be far more tempted to bid on (a), the 13 point hand,
than on (b) with a mere 8 points. In fact, nothing would induce me to bid
on hand (a). The suit is too fragile, and if I am doubled there is no escape.
It could cost a fortune in a most doubtful cause. We have 'soft', potential-
ly defensive points which might be enough to defeat them in a game contract, so why offer them a luscious alternative? It is true to say that players
who bid on hands like this, for one reason or another, often come out
unscathed, but, apart from the fact that even on a good day there is little to
be achieved by such bids, when the axe does fall the carnage will not be a
pretty sight.

Hand (b) is quite a different matter. If they double 2◇, which in any case
seems improbable, good luck to them! Our defensive values are slight and
our playing tricks sound. I very much doubt if they will get value for
money. Furthermore, if partner is on lead we want him to play a diamond.

It is interesting to compare the reactions of the two South players in a
team match when holding these cards at game all:

♠ AQJ108	**West**	**North**	**East**	**South**
♡ AK5	Pass	Pass	Pass	1♠
◇ K64	2◇	2♠	Pass	?
♣ 98				

The bidding started in similar fashion at both tables:

The first South bid a confident 4♠. The second South was inclined to devalue his ◊K and contented himself with a game-try of 3◊. North converted to 3♠ which became the final contract.

Let's see how they got on.

Game All. Dealer West.

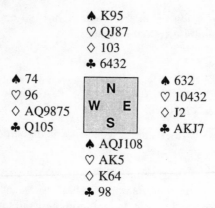

```
              ♠ K95
              ♡ QJ87
              ◊ 103
              ♣ 6432
♠ 74                        ♠ 632
♡ 96        ┌───────┐       ♡ 10432
◊ AQ9875    │ W N E │       ◊ J2
♣ Q105      │   S   │       ♣ AKJ7
            └───────┘
              ♠ AQJ108
              ♡ AK5
              ◊ K64
              ♣ 98
```

Contract: 3♠ by South. Lead: ♡9

As you can see, it was the second South who was successful – he didn't just count his points but reassessed them – as nine tricks proved to be the limit of the hand.

What makes calculating the true value of the points such a difficult task is that a hand can appreciate in value, or slump significantly, rather like a volatile share on the Stock Market. Let's see what you make of this situation. It's game all and you hold:

```
♠ 10863
♡ KJ5
◊ 10763
♣ J10
```

Your partner opens 1♣ (natural) and you drudge up 1♠. He now rebids 2♡ (forcing for one round). For better or for worse, you continue with 2NT which gets 4♡ from your partner. Would you do any more?

This was the full deal:

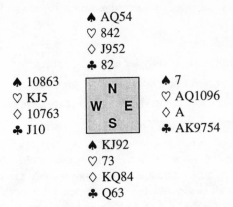

```
                    ♠ AQ54
                    ♡ 842
                    ◇ J952
                    ♣ 82
    ♠ 10863        ┌─────────┐      ♠ 7
    ♡ KJ5          │    N    │      ♡ AQ1096
    ◇ 10763        │ W     E │      ◇ A
    ♣ J10          │    S    │      ♣ AK9754
                   └─────────┘
                    ♠ KJ92
                    ♡ 73
                    ◇ KQ84
                    ♣ Q63
```

The player in the West seat advanced to 5♡, feeling that the doubleton ♣J10 plus good hearts might be enough for slam. How right she was! I was glad to be given a further opportunity and the decision to bid six was easy enough. So, too, was the play.

West's bid of 5♡ seems a very fine effort to me, upgrading a poor hand to its full potential and refusing to be intimidated by the shortage of points

Summary

1. While distribution will always be a strong factor, intermediate cards like tens and nines, and even eights, add substantially to the value of a hand.

   Case for upgrading.

2. Aces are slightly undervalued and a hand improves with the addition of aces. Add one point if holding all four aces.

   Case for upgrading.

3. An aceless hand can prove to be the downfall of an otherwise sound contract, especially in no trumps when the opponents start with their long suit and then have the aces to get in with to win the race.

   Case for downgrading.

4. Depending on the bidding, some unsupported honour cards should be upgraded if they blend with partner's hand, or appear to lie favourably. However, if they are badly placed, a downward adjustment may be necessary.

   Case for upgrading or downgrading.

5. Singleton honours, unsupported honour cards and all 'soft' points should be regarded in a possible minus light, e.g. K, Q, J, KQ, QJ, Jx, Qxx, Jxx.

   Case for downgrading.

6. If the high cards are in your long suit, the playing potential is high.

   Case for upgrading when you are hoping to play.

7. If the high cards are in short suits, the defensive potential is good.

   Case for upgrading if you are going to defend.

8. When considering an intervention – especially at favourable vulnerability – it is the quality of your suit rather than x number of points that really matters. Not having the odd Qx on the side may be an asset when you bid. With defensive values and a doubtful suit – err on the side of caution and downgrade the hand. With a good suit, especially a good six-carder – it's often right to bid.

   Upgrade the hand.

The next most popular method of hand evaluation is of enormous value in assessing the worth of distributional hands. The Losing Trick Count is an invaluable tool to add to your bag.

The Losing Trick Count

Star Rating: ✳✳✳✳

The Losing Trick Count (LTC) is a method of hand valuation that is especially useful (I am tempted to say only useful), when a fit has been located. While no trump type hands that are balanced in nature lend themselves ideally to a point-count method of calculation, the same cannot be said of strongly distributional hands that incorporate a good fit.

The LTC is based on the premise that each hand has a maximum of twelve losers, the ace, king and queen in each suit (cards beyond three in a suit do not count as losers), so that the maximum number of losers between your hand and partner's is 24. Thus, by deducting the actual number of losers that you and your partner have from the key figure of 24, you arrive at the number of tricks you can expect to make. There cannot be more losers in a suit than there are cards. Thus, x and xx represent one and two losers respectively.

A minimum opening hand usually consists of seven losers. Here is an everyday example:

♠ 84		♠ KQ	**West**	**East**
♡ AK753	**N**	♡ Q1084	1♡	4♡
◇ K82	**W E**	◇ QJ53	Pass	
♣ A74	**S**	♣ K92		

West has seven losers (two in spades, one in hearts, two in diamonds and two in clubs). East also has seven losers (one in spades, two each in hearts, diamonds and clubs). Total = 14. Deduct from 24 and you get the answer 10. That is the number of tricks you would expect to make providing there are normal breaks and your finesses are right half the time.

A more shapely example:

♠ 2		♠ J5	**West**	**East**
♡ AK9643	**N**	♡ J1072	1♡	3♡
◇ A1065	**W E**	◇ 84	4♡	Pass
♣ 53	**S**	♣ AK1064		

Opener has only six losers, despite his lack of high-card points, so, when responder raises to 3♡ (eight losers), he bids the game.

We have seen that with seven losers and a fit responder raises to game (1♡–4♡). Let us see how lesser and better values fit into the scenario.

Responder raises opener's suit

Opener	Responder	Responder's losers	Responder's points inc. distribution
1♠	2♠	Usually 9 (maybe 10)	6-9
1♠	3♠	Usually 8	10-12
1♠	4♠	Usually 7	13-14

If responder has fewer losers, six or five, he will usually be able to proceed via another route.

Opener raises responder's suit

Opener	Responder	Opener's losers	Opener's points inc. distribution
1◇ 2♠	1♠	Usually 7 (maybe 6)	13-15
1◇ 3♠	1♠	Usually 6 (maybe 5)	16-18
1◇ 4♠	1♠	Usually 5	19-20

If opener has less than five losers, he will usually be able to proceed by a different route. This may also apply to some hands with five losers, where a jump cuebid or splinter would be more appropriate than a direct raise.

So, is it really just a case of putting a coin into the slot machine and punching out a ticket that tells you precisely what you can make? No, of course it is not as easy as that. What the LTC will do is to point you in the right direction. Then, it will be up to you to assess fitting cards, wastage, controls and so forth. But at least you will have some solid data on which to base your decisions. Let us see if we can sharpen our tools.

The following combinations are worthy of study.

x or **xx**	Clearly one or two losers respectively.
Qx	This holding counts as two losers, but obviously must be afforded a plus value (unless the opposition have bid the suit) as opposite AKx, KJx, AJx, Kx etc., it may be invaluable.
AJx or **KJx**	Although there are two losers in each case the presence of the jack must warrant a plus value.
K or **Q**	If this singleton honour is in partner's suit it is certainly not correct to view it as one loser. A strong plus value.
J10x	This holding may well be better than xxx and warrants a plus in partner's suit.
AJ10	This combination should be counted as only one loser unless partner is known to be short in the suit.
Qxx	This holding calls for special treatment. To count it as two losers is an oversimplification. It is better to think of it as two and a half losers.

Now consider:

(a)	AKJ	AQJ	AQ10	AKJ10	AQJ10
(b)	AKx	AQx	AQx	AKJx	AQJx

Although at basic level there is one loser in each of these combinations the presence of the jack or ten adds considerable playing strength. Count a plus value if you hold any of the combinations denoted (a). In the last two examples in (b) the jack has already provided a plus value but clearly adding the ten makes for an even stronger combination.

When to deduct a loser

1. Deduct a loser when you strike an extra rich trump fit, usually five or six cards in partner's suit.

2. Deduct a loser with hands rich in aces and kings – especially aces.

♠ AJ96
♡ A84
◇ AKJ107
♣ 3

You open 1◇ and hear partner bid 1♠. It would now be appropriate to treat this as a five-loser hand, not six.

Even when the LTC tells you that you can make a slam, it is always necessary to check up on controls. Suppose you are West and hold:

♠ AQ10754
♡ A6
◇ Q
♣ KQ95

You open 1♠, which partner raises to 4♠. That looks promising. Partner is showing you seven losers and you have only four. That suggests a grand slam – if all the controls are present. Cautiously you trot out the 'Old Black' and receive the disappointing reply of 5♣. There is nothing for it but to retreat to 5♠, and, when dummy goes down, you are at least thankful that you didn't get a rush of blood to the head!

These are the two hands:

♠ AQ10754	**N**	♠ KJ862
♡ A6	**W E**	♡ K4
◇ Q	**S**	◇ KJ75
♣ KQ95		♣ 32

The other side of the coin is when you pick up a hand like this:

♠ K10873
♡ A4
◇ Q5
♣ J973

East, your partner, opens the bidding with 1◇. You respond 1♠, which East raises to 3♠. How would you react to that?

Without any cultured adjustment, West has eight losers plain and simple. East has shown six losers which means that West should make ten tricks in spades – all things being equal. Is there a case for being more ambitious? If we count our points, no. If, however, we make allowances for the possibility of right cards (RCS – Right Cards Syndrome) then we might perhaps permit ourselves one try. After all, we have counted two losers for the ♢Q5, which, in view of East's opening bid, may be unduly cautious, if not downright unimaginative. So we make our try with 4♡. Partner bids 5♢ and we pull down the shutters with 5♠, feeling confident that we have left nothing unbid. Partner does not share our feelings, however, and continues to 6♠.

The two hands:

♠ K10873	♠ AQ54
♡ A4	♡ 532
♢ Q5	♢ AKJ103
♣ J973	♣ 4

Although, perhaps, balanced hands with quite a few points may be slightly undervalued by LTC, and shapely features exaggerated a little, the salutary warning on the one hand, and the enthusiastic suggestion on the other, will often guide LTC addicts to the right contract. Let us see.

♠ AK974	♠ QJ85	West	East
♡ A83	♡ Q64	1♠	2♠
♢ J75	♢ A62	Pass	
♣ K8	♣ J74		

Despite the relatively high point count, East can do no more than raise his partner to two spades (nine losers). With seven losers himself, West is not tempted to proceed. So the partnership stays on firm ground.

Then, there is the other side of the coin where the shapely element is allowed full rein:

♠ K98653	♠ QJ72	West	East
♡ A	♡ 873	1♠	3♠(i)
♢ A4	♢ KQ965	4♣(ii)	4♢(iii)
♣ A762	♣ 8	4♡(iv)	5♣(v)
		6♠	

(i) East has seven losers but the point-count is low in an aceless hand so he is content to raise to three spades.

(ii) West's controls could hardly be better. It wouldn't be outrageous to jump to 6♠ immediately (five losers minus one for aces = four, plus eight losers makes twelve. 24 − 12 = 12 tricks) but he settles for the cuebid (see chapter 3).

(iii) East does not want to sign off so he compromises with 4◇.

(iv) and (v) are cuebids and West settles happily for the small slam.

Success on a joint holding of 23 points can't be too bad.

I am going to conclude with a hand from the 1989 European Championships. It occurred in the Women's Series, Germany v Netherlands.

East/West Game. Dealer West.

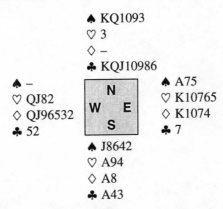

```
                  ♠ KQ1093
                  ♡ 3
                  ◇ −
                  ♣ KQJ10986
   ♠ −                          ♠ A75
   ♡ QJ82          N            ♡ K10765
   ◇ QJ96532    W     E         ◇ K1074
   ♣ 52             S            ♣ 7
                  ♠ J8642
                  ♡ A94
                  ◇ A8
                  ♣ A43
```

In one room, without opposition bidding, the North/South pair bid smoothly to six spades. There was plenty of time and all the relevant questions got answered. Well done.

In the other room this was the bidding:

West	North	East	South
Pass	1♣	1♡	1♠
4♡	4♠	All Pass	

Of course, twelve tricks were made without pausing for breath, but what should one make of that bidding sequence? On this occasion the East/West bidding took up a lot of space and left little room for manoeuvre. East/West were vulnerable and were presumably not bidding on peanuts. Even so, North had only three losers and wouldn't be completely happy about bidding four spades. Still, if South were minimum and unsuitable then the five level might be over the top.

How about South? She has eight losers, it is true, but an opening bid and three aces plus five trumps seems to suggest suitable cards (RCS again). Ardent fans of LTC might proceed via five clubs, but any move would obviously hit the jackpot.

Perhaps this brings us back to where we came in. All our guides and props can steer us in the right direction, but in the final analysis it comes down to our own judgement.

2
BIDDING TO GAME

Trial Bids

Star Rating: ✳✳✳✳

After partner has raised your major suit to the two level (1♡–2♡) do you ever wonder whether you should play it safe and pass, jump to game and hope for the best, or perhaps just continue with your suit to the three level (1♡–2♡–3♡) and hope partner can sort it out? And if you are the partner trying to sort it out do you ever wonder what to do? If you never have any problem in these situations I suggest you turn the page and read something else. Alternatively, stay with me. There is an (almost) magic formula that can save you many a future headache.

Suppose you open 1♡ holding:

♠ 84
♡ AQJ65
♢ A854
♣ A3

Your partner raises to 2♡ and RHO passes. What would you do now?

Clearly you have some hope of making game if your partner holds the right cards – and very little hope if he holds the wrong ones. If you simply raise the ante to 3♡, how is partner to know whether he has what you require, or whether his values are largely wasted? Playing Trial Bids you don't bid 3♡ and you've no need to guess; you just bid three in the suit where you want help, in this case 3♢.

So, a Trial Bid is a change of suit after a major suit has been raised to the two level. Although, perhaps, a Trial Bid is more likely to be initiated by the opener (1♠–2♠–3♢) responder can also initiate a Trial Bid; for example after 1♣–1♡ –2♡ he might bid 2♠.

The Trial Bid is an invitation to game in the agreed major suit. It consists of three or more cards (usually three or four) in the suit where help is most wanted. For example, 1♠–2♠–3◊ means: 'I am interested in four spades, and need help in diamonds'. Always choose a weak suit for your Trial Bid, typically a suit with two or three losers. If there are two trial suits from which to choose, go for the weaker. If the suits are equal, select the cheaper. Don't make a Trial Bid in a suit with only one loser.

When to Make a Trial Bid

After 1♡–2♡, or 1♠–2♠, opener makes a Trial Bid on a hand where he can't quite be sure whether a game is on or not; this will normally be a hand with about 16-18 points (including distributional points) or a hand with six losers. If opener has seven losers, about 12-15 points, it will usually be right to pass, whereas if he has only five losers, about 19-20 points including distributional points, he will be able to bid game without searching for more information.

Responder's raise to the two level in partner's major (1♠–2♠) shows around nine losers – sometimes eight, sometimes ten.

After responder has been raised to the two level in his major (1◊–1♠ –2♠) he may make a Trial Bid with about 10-12 points – again, including distribution. This will usually mean about seven to eight losers. It is true that opener will more often than not have seven losers, but he may have something extra – six losers with a minimum point count – or, even more pertinent, his values may be just where they are needed. That is what Trial Bids are all about. Are partner's goodies in the right place to eliminate enough of your losers?

Sometimes responder – and occasionally opener – may envisage a slam after his suit has been raised to the two level. When this happens he can then use a Trial Bid to discover whether partner can help in the trial suit. Depending on the reply the trial bidder continues to game or slam.

Replying to the Trial Bid – the (almost) Magic Formula

If you have no losers in the trial suit – jump to game in the agreed major.

If you have one loser in the trial suit – jump to game in the agreed major.

If you have two losers in the trial suit – jump to game in the agreed major if maximum. Sign off in three of the agreed major if minimum.

If you have three losers in the trial suit – sign off in three of the agreed major, even when maximum.

Let us look at some hands.

Game All. Dealer South.

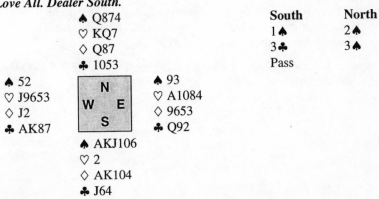

```
                 ♠ 9763
                 ♡ K974
                 ◇ K6
                 ♣ 762
  ♠ AKQ        N           ♠ J1052
  ♡ 1083    W     E        ♡ 2
  ◇ J7                     ◇ Q10932
  ♣ J9854      S           ♣ KQ10
                 ♠ 84
                 ♡ AQJ65
                 ◇ A854
                 ♣ A3
```

South	North
1♡	2♡
3◇	4♡
Pass	

When North raises opener's 1♡ to 2♡, South is in something of a dilemma. His hand is worth about 17 points (15 + 1 point for each doubleton after trump agreement) and he has exactly six losers. North is likely to have about nine losers which in isolation suggests a part-score, not game. However, if North can help in diamonds the 'right cards syndrome' may bridge the gap. So South introduces a Trial Bid with 3◇ and North, employing the (almost) magic formula, jumps to game as he has only one loser in the trial suit (Ax, Kx or x count as one loser).

The play is Momma-Poppa. West leads three top spades and declarer ruffs the third round. Now all he has to do is ensure that he ruffs his two losing diamonds in dummy before drawing all the trumps. The easiest plan is to cash the ◇A and ◇K and ruff a diamond. Return to hand with a high trump and ruff a second diamond. The rest is plain sailing.

Love All. Dealer South.

```
                 ♠ Q874
                 ♡ KQ7
                 ◇ Q87
                 ♣ 1053
  ♠ 52          N           ♠ 93
  ♡ J9653    W     E        ♡ A1084
  ◇ J2                      ◇ 9653
  ♣ AK87       S            ♣ Q92
                 ♠ AKJ106
                 ♡ 2
                 ◇ AK104
                 ♣ J64
```

South	North
1♠	2♠
3♣	3♠
Pass	

After 1♠–2♠ South has every reason to be interested in game. 16 HCPs plus two for distribution give him a total of eighteen points and, of course, he has a six-loser hand. The doubt lies in just where North's high cards are situated. The Trial Bid of 3♣ soon gets the thumbs down (North has three losers in clubs) and the partnership stay in a safe partscore. Interchange North's club and heart holding and the (almost) magic formula would dictate that North rebid 4♠, which would then be easy.

Two suited hands that fit well always play for a lot of tricks.

Consider:

Game All. Dealer South.

		South	North
♠ 10865		1♡	2♡
♡ Q854		3◇	4♡
◇ KQ5		6♡	Pass
♣ 86			

```
        ♠ 10865
        ♡ Q854
        ◇ KQ5
        ♣ 86
♠ KJ32    ┌───────┐   ♠ AQ94
♡ 96      │   N   │   ♡ 72
◇ 106     │ W   E │   ◇ 742
♣ KQ1042  │   S   │   ♣ 9753
          └───────┘
        ♠ 7
        ♡ AKJ103
        ◇ AJ983
        ♣ AJ
```

South realised that he had plenty of ammunition for a direct jump to game after North's raise to 2♡. However, before committing himself to a modest game contract, he decided to try the effect of a Trial Bid of 3◇. North's jump to 4♡ got South's adrenalin going and he decided to risk the slam. In the event twelve tricks were virtually lay-down (five hearts, five diamonds, one club and one club ruff in dummy).

Although the cards lay poorly on the next hand North/South bid and made a thin game which was not duplicated in the other room.

East/West Game. IMPs. Dealer West.

```
                ♠ K1052
                ♡ 7
                ◇ AJ1094
                ♣ K104
  ♠ QJ7          ┌───────┐      ♠ 9
  ♡ KQJ8         │   N   │      ♡ 109432
  ◇ 87           │ W   E │      ◇ KQ5
  ♣ 7632         │   S   │      ♣ A985
                 └───────┘
                ♠ A8643
                ♡ A65
                ◇ 652
                ♣ QJ
```

South	North
–	1◇
1♠	2♠
3♡	4♠
Pass	

North had nothing to spare when he opened the bidding with 1◇ and raised his partner's 1♠ to 2♠. However, South had the points to make an effort although he was rather heavy with losers. In any case he decided to make a Trial Bid with 3♡ and then the (almost) magic formula was duly applied by North – one loser in hearts meant a jump to game in the agreed major – and so they arrived.

Even with both diamonds offside and the spades failing to break South was not severely tested. He won the opening heart lead, ruffed a heart, played a club to his queen, East ducking, and ruffed his last heart. Now the ♠K and ♠A were followed by the ♣J to establish a diamond discard. So the opponents made just one spade, one club and one diamond.

There are two final points to consider. What do these sequences mean?

(i)	1♡	2♡	*or*	1♠	2♠
	2NT			2NT	

(ii)	1♡	2♡	*or*	1♠	2♠
	3♡			3♠	

(i) The first is fairly easy. It is a Trial Bid on a balanced hand of about 17-18 points. Something like this:

```
                ♠ AQ106
                ♡ KJ5
                ◇ AJ103
                ♣ Q104
```

Partner can pass, raise, sign off in 3♠ or jump to 4♠.

(ii) Interpretation of this sequence depends on partnership agreement. In some circles it will have a natural meaning: 'I am interested in game but have no particular suit that I want to introduce as a Trial Bid. If you are maximum, go to game. If you are minimum, pass.' That is a perfectly playable arrangement.

Indeed, suppose you hold:

> ♠ QJ1084
> ♡ KJ10
> ◇ AK5
> ♣ K6

and open 1♠ which partner raises to 2♠. What now? Playing three spades as a general try you are in business. Partner can assess his hand fairly accurately. That, very briefly, is the case for the constructive raise.

The alternative treatment of 1♡–2♡–3♡ or 1♠–2♠–3♠ is based on a weak hand. The thinking is this: 'If I pass after this sequence (1♡–2♡) my Left Hand Opponent is almost certain to re-open, and as we have a fit and are not very strong, they are sure to find a playable spot – perhaps even make a game – so I will do my best to make life difficult for them. Even if I end up one over the top it may still be a good result.'

Here is an example:

♠ 5	♠ Q74	West	East
♡ AJ9864	♡ K752	1♡	2♡
◇ KQ10	◇ 9843	3♡	Pass
♣ J74	♣ Q8		

I must admit that I am very biased about the merits of these two treatments. I prefer the latter, which budgets for weak hands with a fit. My feeling is that strong hands will often look after themselves while weak hands need wrapping up. Sometimes even camouflaging. So, is it to be the heavy artillery or the machine gun? While I have made it clear that I prefer the machine gun (one, two, three – shut them up), other views have to be respected.

All I suggest is that you sort it out with your partner so that you both know what you are doing. In any event I hope I have made out a powerful case for Trial Bids which all good players acknowledge are invaluable.

The Delayed Game Raise

Star Rating: ✳✳✳✳

In the early days of a bridge player's life it is never easy to get them to support partner. The natural instinct is to paint a pretty little picture and let the future take care of itself (with ♠xx ♡Qxxx ◇AQJxx ♣xx they will all bid 2◇ over partner's 1♡ instead of raising to 3♡.) Then, just as you've got them to raise major suits quantitatively, without stopping to pick the flowers or paint pretty pictures, you start introducing hands where it is clearly advantageous to – do just that. All very confusing.

What it boils down to is this. There are five main types of reply you can make when you have length and values in partner's major suit:

(i) Raise partner quantitatively: 1♠–2♠; 1♠–3♠; 1♠–4♠.

(ii) Show your own suit first and then leap to game on the next round, e.g.:

(a)	1♡	1♠
	1NT	4♡
(b)	1♡	2♣
	2NT	4♡
(c)	1♡	2♣
	2◇	4♡

(iii) Jump in a new suit and support partner on the next round:

(a)	1♡	2♠
	3♣	3♡
(b)	1♠	3◇
	3♡	3♠
(c)	1♡	3♣
	3NT	4♡
(d)	1♡	2♠
	3♡	4♡

(iv) Use Swiss. See Chapter 4.

(v) Use a Splinter Bid. See Chapter 4.

Let us try and differentiate between the first three. Partner opens one heart and you hold:

(a) ♠ 4   (b) ♠ A108   (c) ♠ A10
    ♡ K10964   ♡ KJ83   ♡ KJ83
    ◊ KJ875   ◊ KJ1065   ◊ AKJ104
    ♣ 63   ♣ 8   ♣ 84

On Hand (a) you may or may not make four hearts but it is certainly in your interests to get there as quickly as possible. If your opponents now want to start bidding they can do so at the four level. It is by no means uncommon in these situations to find that while your partner succeeds in making 4♡, the opponents could have made 4♠. Even if 4♡ goes down it may well be in a good cause for at least you have crowded the auction and made it difficult for the opposition to get together. So you can see, this is no occasion to paint pretty pictures.

Hand (b) is a very different proposition. Although anything is possible, you have no reason to fear the opposition. It is most unlikely that you will be outbid so this is the moment to start painting a pretty picture. Bid 2◊ with the intention of leaping to 4♡ on the next round. This is called a Delayed Game Raise, DGR for short.

Hand (c) is much too strong for a DGR so you should jump to 3◊ and then support hearts on the next round. Plenty of time to stop and pick the flowers!

Having shown you a few hands where you want to be in game (at least) opposite partner's opening bid of one of a major, yet requiring a different treatment in each case, I now want to concentrate solely on the DGR.

A DGR hand will have at least four-card support for partner's major. It will have adequate values to go to game and will have sufficient high cards so that you do not fear the opposition. Ideally it will contain a secondary suit of some substance, and in terms of general acceptability it lies between the hand that raises directly to game and the hand that forces and then supports.

Partner opens 1♡ and you hold:

             (a) ♠ K9
                  ♡ Q1097
                  ◊ AQJ74
                  ♣ 86

Respond 2◊. A fairly typical Delayed Game Raise.

        (b) ♠ A106
              ♡ KJ84
              ◇ 52
              ♣ KQ74

Respond 2♣. A fairly typical Delayed Game Raise.

        (c) ♠ KQ
              ♡ A1094
              ◇ 9642
              ♣ KQ10

Your hand is too strong in top cards to bid four hearts immediately but the diamonds are too weak to mention. Compromise with two clubs where at least you have some values.

Partner opens 1♠ and you hold:

        (a) ♠ K1082
              ♡ AKQJ
              ◇ 6
              ♣ 9764

Respond 2♡. You don't need five as you are eventually going to play in spades. Partner would get the wrong impression if you bid 2♣ and would tend to devalue his hand with, say, a singleton club.

        (b) ♠ AQ85
              ♡ 4
              ◇ KQJ75
              ♣ 642

Respond 2◇. A textbook Delayed Game Raise.

        (c) ♠ KJ74
              ♡ 854
              ◇ KQJ7
              ♣ 42

Respond 3♠. You are not strong enough for 4♠ and therefore must not consider a Delayed Game Raise.

You will notice, perhaps, that in all my examples of the DGR I have purposely avoided having two or more aces in the responding hands. That is because the Swiss convention is all about game-going hands with aces in response to partner's major. Both conventions, the DGR and Swiss, can be used by responder without necessarily clashing, but if I am forced to choose betwen the two I would invariably give preference to Swiss. If you don't play Swiss there is no reason to restrict the number of aces in responder's hand. Let's look at some hands.

Love All. Dealer West.

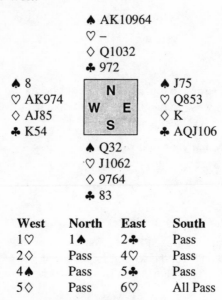

```
                    ♠ AK10964
                    ♡ –
                    ◇ Q1032
                    ♣ 972
    ♠ 8              N          ♠ J75
    ♡ AK974     W       E      ♡ Q853
    ◇ AJ85                      ◇ K
    ♣ K54            S          ♣ AQJ106
                    ♠ Q32
                    ♡ J1062
                    ◇ 9764
                    ♣ 83
```

West	North	East	South
1♡	1♠	2♣	Pass
2◇	Pass	4♡	Pass
4♠	Pass	5♣	Pass
5◇	Pass	6♡	All Pass

Although many Easts would 'read' West as probably 5-4 in the red suits and therefore jump to four hearts with any three-card support, West reasoned that his partner had DGR values because he had eschewed a 2♠ enquiry over 2◇ (a bridge player's thinking as opposed to a scientist's assumption). In any case the top cards in the red suits, the club fit and singleton spade all suggested further investigation. The three cuebids that followed confirmed the controls and decided East on the final slam target.

North led the two top spades and the moment of truth arrived as West trumped the second round. Remembering his lessons on precaution plays, West led the ♡7 to dummy's ♡Q and was thus able to pick up all South's trumps without loss. The point is this. If North holds all four trumps nothing can be done to avoid the loss of one trump trick, but if South holds them it is essential to play to the single honour first. Give East the ♡10 instead of a small one and then declarer must first cash one of the top honours from his own hand.

It sometimes happens that opener rebids his own major suit thus thwarting responder's plan to paint a DGR picture with his first rebid. If the bidding starts 1♡–2◇–2♡ responder would raise to 4♡ with something like this:

```
♠ 75
♡ 1064
◇ AKJ842
♣ KJ
```

Even if he has DGR values it often won't matter because if partner can only rebid his suit at the lowest level nothing will be missed. But suppose instead he holds a highly suitable DGR hand:

```
♠ 7
♡ K1064
◇ AKJ105
♣ Q103
```

would he make the same rebid of 4♡? Let's see how East coped with a similar situation on the following hand:

Game All. Dealer South.

	♠ 2		West	East
	♡ AJ10532		1♠	2◇
	◇ 86		2♠	3♣
	♣ J942		3◇	4♠
♠ AK9754	N	♠ QJ83	5♣	5♡
♡ 86	W E	♡ 7	6♠	Pass
◇ Q94	S	◇ AK1073		
♣ A5		♣ K83		
	♠ 106			
	♡ KQ94			
	◇ J52			
	♣ Q1076			

East started on an informative DGR sequence with his bid of 2◇ intending to leap to 4♠ on the next round. However, when West rebid 2♠ East decided on a different tack. 3♣ was forcing (a new suit at the three level) and provided just the opportunity he was looking for when West rebid 3◇. The leap to game now instead of on the previous round made West realise that he might have the right cards for slam. The heart cuebid over 5♣ reinforced this impression so West bid the slam which turned out to be lay-down.

When you have a misfit with partner's first suit it is generally wise to undervalue your hand somewhat, unless there are strong redeeming features.

West thought he had these features on the following hand:

North/South Game. Dealer West.

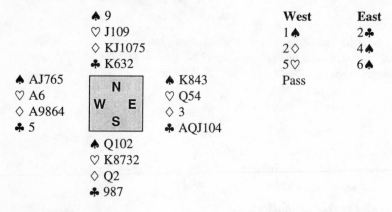

	♠ 9		**West**	**East**
	♡ J109		1♠	2♣
	◇ KJ1075		2◇	4♠
	♣ K632		5♡	6♠
♠ AJ765		♠ K843	Pass	
♡ A6		♡ Q54		
◇ A9864		◇ 3		
♣ 5		♣ AQJ104		
	♠ Q102			
	♡ K8732			
	◇ Q2			
	♣ 987			

Despite his singleton club, West liked his shape and three aces and decided the best 'urge' was 5♡. East did not take much urging. He could either sign off in 5♠ or bid the slam. With nothing to be ashamed of, he went for gold.

North led the ♡J, covered by the queen, king and ace. West realised he had plenty on his plate and would need a little luck if he were to be successful. The first move was a club to the ♣A followed by the ♣Q for a ruffing finesse. North won but West was able to discard his losing heart and now, hopefully, there were three discards for declarer's losing diamonds, and the fourth could be trumped in dummy. The heart continuation was ruffed leaving just the problem of how to play the trump suit. West could not afford a wrong guess. A spade to the ♠K caught the ♠9 from North and the ♠2 from South. On the next spade from dummy South played the ♠10 and there was an agonising trance before West guessed correctly by playing the ♠J. With one singleton in dummy and one in his own hand, declarer thought that North might perhaps have one as well – and so it proved. West made five spades, four clubs, the two red aces and a diamond ruff, totalling twelve tricks.

Despite West's success on this hand, it is generally right to view misfits pessimistically, while taking an optimistic view of hands that knit well together.

Fourth Suit Forcing

Star Rating: ✻✻✻✻✻

Ask a bridge expert what he considers the most useful contribution to bidding theory in the last thirty to forty years, and, as likely as not, he will answer 'Fourth Suit Forcing'. Indeed, so useful is this development, and so efficient its application, that one cannot help wondering how on earth the good bidders of the pre-FSF era ever managed without it. Good judgement, good bridge sense, or just a nose for diagnosing the problem? Whatever it was, they did pretty well, but no-one would deny that they would have done even better with the addition of FSF to their armoury.

This is a typical everyday problem. You are East and hold:

	West	East
♠ A93		
♡ KJ1074	1♢	1♡
♢ AQ	1♠	?
♣ 632		

You now have an almost insoluble problem – unless you are playing FSF. You have the points to go to game, but which game? Four hearts, four spades, 3NT, five diamonds? Bids like 3♡, 3♠ and 3♢ are all non-forcing so they must be discarded. 3♣ would be forcing, of course, but it certainly wouldn't be descriptive. The answer is to use a bid at the lowest level in the one remaining unbid suit as an artificial forcing bid. As the other three suits have been bid by your side, you can see why this convention is called fourth suit forcing. This bid asks partner for further clarification. It is forcing and does not guarantee any strength in the suit at all. After all, if your clubs were strong in the above hand (interchange the clubs and diamonds, for example) you would rebid 3NT as you would have no reason to ask any further questions.

It might be helpful to look at a few possible hands that West might hold consistent with the bidding (1♢-1♡-1♠-2♣) so far.

(a) ♠ K754	(b) ♠ KQ54	(c) ♠ KQ54
♡ 63	♡ AQ2	♡ A
♢ KJ1053	♢ KJ532	♢ KJ10532
♣ AQ	♣ 8	♣ 84

On Hand (a) West will rebid 2NT and East will continue to 3NT. If the West hand were a little stronger, say the ♡Q instead of a small one, West would go direct to 3NT himself.

On Hand (b) West will rebid 3♡ and that should pave the way to the small slam in hearts. With a minimum hand, say ♡QJ2 instead of ♡AQ2, West should rebid 2♡ which will lead to a final contract of 4♡.

On Hand (c) West will rebid his diamonds leading to a final contract of 5◇.

Notice how easy it is to head in the right direction after the fourth suit has been introduced and how guesswork is almost completely eliminated. Although responder is more likely to want to use FSF than opener the bid is nevertheless available to both partners.

Suppose as West you deal and hold:

	West	East
♠ KJ4		
♡ AK975	1♡	2♣
◇ 863	2♡	2♠
♣ A4	?	

Now, surely, your best bid is 3◇ – the fourth suit asking for further clarification. Certainly you can't bid 3NT with three small diamonds (although East might be happy to do so) and it would be premature to be too demonstrative about the other three suits. However, let us concentrate on responder's FSF bid as that is probably where the bulk of the action lies.

There are a number of questions that need answering.

   (a) How strong do you have to be to introduce a FSF bid?
   (b) Which replies by partner are still forcing?
   (c) When should you avoid a FSF bid?

(a) Obviously if responder has game-going values he is on firm ground when demanding further information. Also, when just short of an opening bid himself, say about 11-12 points or even a promising ten count, he may best be served by enquiring further.

(b) If the FSF bid is made at the three level this creates a game-forcing situation. If it is made at the two level, opener's minimum rebid can be passed. For example:

West	East
1◇	1♡
1♠	2♣ (FSF)
?	

Now rebids of 2◇, 2♡ or 2NT are all non-forcing (2♠ would be forcing) so clearly opener should avoid making a minimum reply to FSF with 15 or more points. Any jump bid after FSF is forcing to game. However, any further bid responder makes short of game is still forcing. For example:

West	East
1♡	1♠
2♣	2◇ (FSF)
2♡	3♣
?	

This last bid is still forcing. With a weaker hand East would simply have raised 2♣ to 3♣ without using the FSF bid of 2◇.

(c) Never use FSF if you have a natural clearcut bid that you can make instead. Study these examples. You hold as East:

(i)

♠ AJ742
♡ KJ10
◇ 8642
♣ 5

West	East
1♡	1♠
2♣	?

Bid 3♡. A jump preference, limit bid.

(ii)

♠ AJ10
♡ KQ104
◇ 72
♣ QJ53

West	East
1◇	1♡
2♣	?

Bid 3NT. You have enough information.

(iii)

♠ AJ9743
♡ Q5
◇ K1096
♣ QJ53

West	East
1◇	1♠
2♡	?

Bid 4◇. This bid is forcing and paves the way for further investigation. It would be pointless, and muddling, to introduce the fourth suit.

(iv)

♠ Q64
♡ AQ6
◇ K953
♣ A72

West	East
1♠	2◇
2♡	?

Here there is no obvious bid to make; you do need more information. So bid 3♣, FSF, you will see what actually happened later.

Action by opener after partner bids the fourth suit

You hold as West:

(a)	♠ QJ105	**West**	**East**
	♡ 6	1◇	1♡
	◇ AQJ74	1♠	2♣
	♣ K105	?	

Bid 2NT. You have a club stop and you are minimum. With, say, the ♠A instead of the ♠Q you would bid 3NT.

(b)	♠ KJ5	**West**	**East**
	♡ AK843	1♡	1♠
	◇ 5	2♣	2◇
	♣ AJ105	?	

Bid 3♠ – forcing to game. With a small spade instead of the ♠K you would bid 2♠.

(c)	♠ AK84	**West**	**East**
	♡ 3	1◇	1♡
	◇ AKJ1063	1♠	2♣
	♣ 82	?	

Jump to 3◇ – forcing to game.

(d)	♠ A1086	**West**	**East**
	♡ AK74	1♣	1◇
	◇ –	1♡	1♠
	♣ KQJ86	?	

Raise to 3♠ – forcing to game. Although you have the values to bid 4♠ it would be dangerous to do so because East might not have a spade suit.

Let us look at some full hands:

Love All. Rubber Bridge. Dealer North.

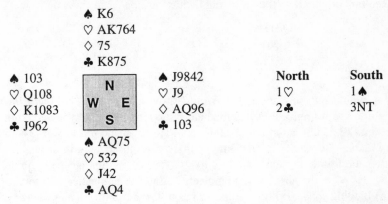

♠ K6
♡ AK764
◇ 75
♣ K875

♠ 103
♡ Q108
◇ K1083
♣ J962

♠ J9842
♡ J9
◇ AQ96
♣ 103

♠ AQ75
♡ 532
◇ J42
♣ AQ4

North	South
1♡	1♠
2♣	3NT

Hardly a cultured sequence but nevertheless not too divorced from the real world of rubber bridge where sometimes sophistication is almost regarded as a dirty word.

West led the ◇3 and declarer used up a fair portion of his good luck when the suit divided 4-4. However, he wasn't out of the wood yet. East won the fourth diamond and switched to a spade. Declarer won in dummy, tried the clubs, and and when they didn't break he cashed his spade winners. On the ♠Q West was squeezed. He had to retain the ♣J so he parted with the ♡8. Dummy's club, having done its work, was discarded, and the ♡A, K and 7 took the last three tricks.

So, to make his contract of 3NT South not only had to be lucky with the diamond break, he also had to play well, in that he had to judge the right squeeze to play for. With the use of FSF North/South would have sailed to their right contract of 4♡ and made (at least) ten tricks without difficulty.

North	South
1♡	1♠
2♣	2◇
2♡	4♡

2◇, the fourth suit, asks for clarification and 2♡ denies a diamond stop or three spades. 2♡ is the least helpful bid that North can make; nevertheless it is steeped in truth, and South responds accordingly. East, who hopefully is tuned into the bidding, should lead the ◇A, in which case the defence will make two diamonds and a trump. Playing pairs, North/South would be extremely grateful that they had FSF in their armoury of bids.

My last hand demonstrates a further extension of the FSF principle. Remember, you held the following hand as responder in c (iv) on page 37:

		West	East
♠ Q64		**West**	**East**
♡ AQ6		1♠	2◇
◇ K953		2♡	?
♣ A72			

4♠ would not be right as that would show a DGR, and although East could have responded 3NT immediately showing his hand type and point-count (13-15), it is too late for that now. However the fourth suit (3♣) is available. By this time East knows that he wants to play in spades and after the fourth suit there are two likely ways of continuing: (i) by jumping to 4♠ on the next round to indicate that he has completed his story, or (ii) bidding spades without a jump so as to leave room for an exchange of cuebids.

Switching you to the North position for convenience. This was the hand:

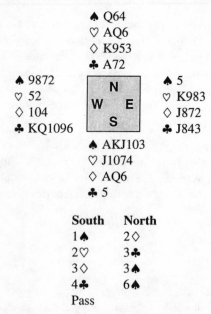

```
                    ♠ Q64
                    ♡ AQ6
                    ◇ K953
                    ♣ A72
        ♠ 9872                      ♠ 5
        ♡ 52         N              ♡ K983
        ◇ 104      W   E            ◇ J872
        ♣ KQ1096     S              ♣ J843
                    ♠ AKJ103
                    ♡ J1074
                    ◇ AQ6
                    ♣ 5
```

South	North
1♠	2◇
2♡	3♣
3◇	3♠
4♣	6♠
Pass	

There was no problem in the play, twelve tricks being an easy make, but the declarer at this table was a happier man than his opposite number. At the other table the final contract rested in 4♠ after a less informative sequence.

3
BIDDING TO SLAM

Slams are one of the most exciting aspects of bridge. Bidding a hand to the six level, or, even better, to seven, and then garnering the requisite number of tricks is one of a bridge player's biggest thrills. Unfortunately, there is a downside. Going down in a high-level contract is an enormous fillip to the opposition and can be very expensive for your own chances of winning. It is an area where all players can improve their performance overnight. This chapter aims to show you some of the tricks of the trade.

Cuebidding

Star Rating:✳✳✳✳✳

A cuebid is one of the most useful gadgets in the whole field of bidding and while it is worshipped by experts, to the extent that most would willingly forgo almost anything else provided they were allowed to retain their favourite toy, the novice is deeply suspicious of having anything to do with it. Indeed, only recently I came across a couple far removed from novice class – in fact they played a fair, average game – who astonished me by saying 'We never use cuebids. We don't really understand them.' That's rather like a doubles player at tennis saying, 'We never volley. It doesn't suit our game.' My hope is that, having read this book, everybody will be able to understand cuebidding and thus add a formidable weapon to their armoury.

When does a cuebid occur?

A cuebid occurs after suit agreement, invariably at the three or four level, but sometimes at the five level. A new suit, after such agreement, is a cuebid showing slam interest and control of the suit mentioned, e.g.

(a) 1♡	3♡		(b) 1♣	1♠	
4♣				3♠	4◇
(c) 2♡	3♡		(d) 1◇	1♠	
3♠				4♠	5♣

(e) 1NT   3♡
    4◊

The last bid in every sequence is a cuebid. In the sequence 1NT-3♡-4◊ the bid of 4◊ shows the ◊A and agrees hearts by inference – opener could hardly want to play in his diamond suit.

What does a cuebid show?
Initially a cuebid shows first-round control – an ace or void – outside the trump suit. Subsequently, a cuebid shows second-round control – a king or singleton – outside the trump suit.

A cuebidder always bids his controls up-the-line, the cheapest first, e.g.

West	East
1♡	3♡
4♣	

West's bid of 4♣ denies the ♠A. Equally, should East continue with 4♠ he would be denying the ◊A.

What is the purpose of a cuebid?
A cuebid shows interest in slam, reveals controls and invites partner to cuebid in reply. By pinpointing specific controls a partnership can either stay at a safe level or continue to an excellent slam.

When does the cuebidding end?
A return to the agreed trump suit signifies that that player has no more to show. Otherwise cuebidding continues until one of the partners can tell whether to bid a small slam, a grand slam or reject a slam completely. Don't continue cuebidding if you know that a small slam offers good prospects but a grand slam is impossible. Just bid the small slam. But, if further information is required that could lead to seven – keep cuebidding.

Why bother with cuebids, why not just use Blackwood?
Many hands are just not suitable for a Blackwood 4NT enquiry, as we shall see later. In particular, hands that contain voids or hands with only small cards (no ace or king) in a side-suit do not lend themselves to Blackwood. Blackwood is fine if all you want to know is the number of aces and kings held by partner. When you wish to discover specific controls and shortages then cuebids are the answer.

When is a new suit after (major) suit agreement not a cuebid?
(i) When a major suit is raised to the two level a change of suit is a trial

bid, not a cuebid, e.g. 1♡-2♡-3◇. Opener's bid of 3◇ is a trial bid for game in hearts. See page 23.

(ii) When partner raises your minor suit, bids at the three level should be treated as stoppers for 3NT, not cuebids, e.g. 1♡-2♣-3♣; if responder continues with 3◇ or 3♠ he may be showing just a stopper in the suit bid. In certain circumstances this will enable opener to bid 3NT.

Let us look at the system at work. Suppose as West you hold:

♠ AQJ753
♡ –
◇ J1098
♣ AKJ

You open the bidding with 1♠. Your partner raises you to 3♠. What now? 4♠ might be enough, yet 6♠ might be cold. Blackwood won't answer your problem if partner tells you he holds one ace, because you won't know whether it is the ♡A or ◇A. Indeed, the five level might even be too high. However, you are now well into cuebids so you rebid 4♣ – your lowest first-round control outside the trump suit. If your partner continues with 4♡ or 4♠ you will call it a day and settle for game, but if he shows you the ◇A – now that is quite a different matter.

Here is your hand again, opposite two possible hands that your partner, East, might hold:

West	(a) East	(a) West	East
♠ AQJ753	♠ K1064	1♠	3♠
♡ –	♡ AQ108	4♣	4♡
◇ J1098	◇ 753	4♠	
♣ AKJ	♣ Q9		

	(b) East	(b) West	East
	♠ K1064	1♠	3♠
	♡ 1084	4♣	4◇
	◇ AQ75	4♡	4♠
	♣ Q9	6♠	

When East holds hand (a) the bidding stops in 4♠ – just in time. The news that East holds the ♡A (he has denied the ◇A because he has to bid up-the-line, lowest control first) is bad medicine and West will want to shut up shop with almost indecent haste.

When East holds hand (b) he is able to cuebid 4♦ over 4♣ and that is really exciting news for West. Caught up in the euphoria of the moment, West continues with 4♡, although it is almost impossible for East to have the right cards for a grand slam (remember he made the limit bid of 3♠ over 1♠). Maybe West visualises something like ♠Kxxx ♡xxxxx ♦AK ♣xx. Not to worry, East has to sign off in 4♠ but West already knows that the small slam must be heavy odds on so heads right there to close the auction. Maybe West was lucky to find the ♦Q in the East hand, but even without this card the small slam is still a tremendous bet. There are no bridge players with red blood in their veins who would not wish to be in a small slam if success depended on nothing worse than losing only one trick in a suit consisting of J1098 opposite Axxx – in isolation a 76% chance.

Once more you are West and hold:

West	(a) East	(b) East
♠ AQ	♠ KJ9	♠ KJ9
♡ AK843	♡ QJ1072	♡ QJ107
♦ 65	♦ J10	♦ AJ104
♣ KQ93	♣ AJ4	♣ J4

You open 1♡ and on both hands (a) and (b) East raises you to 4♡. Glancing across to East we see that each hand contains thirteen points but whereas (a) has five trumps (b) has only four. Nevertheless with hand (a) there is no play for 6♡. With hand (b), however, 6♡ is virtually ironclad. So how should the bidding go? Firstly you must dismiss any idea of Blackwood. The reply won't help you.

Then you launch yourself into a cuebidding sequence:

(a) West	East		(b) West	East
1♡	4♡		1♡	4♡
4♠	5♣		4♠	5♦
5♡			6♡	

West makes his first move with 4♠, cuebidding the ♠A and inviting a cuebid in return. With hand (a) East duly obliges with 5♣ but without diamond control himself West has to sign off in 5♡. With hand (b) East denies the ♣A when he responds 5♦. This is exactly what West wants to hear. With all suits controlled and expecting a sufficiency of tricks on the bidding he has no hesitation in contracting for the small slam.

Study the following hands and sequences with West as dealer.

♠ AKJ96		♠ Q1084	West	East
♡ 4	N	♡ 1053	1♠	3♠
◇ AKQ92	W E	◇ J8	4◇	5♣
♣ 83	S	♣ AK65	6♠	

West knows there are plenty of tricks available but cannot be sure about club control. Blackwood would not solve his problem but a cuebid and return cuebid provide the answer.

♠ Q1085		♠ AK9762	West	East
♡ KQJ72	N	♡ A4	1♡	1♠
◇ AQ	W E	◇ J853	3♠	4♡
♣ Q9	S	♣ 2	5◇	6♠

Once East knows about diamond control he is not bothered that the ♣A is missing. The bidding indicates that there should be enough tricks available.

♠ A1075		♠ –	West	East
♡ A63	N	♡ 74	1NT	3◇
◇ 84	W E	◇ AKQ1075	3NT	4♣
♣ A987	S	♣ KJ1063	4♡	6♣

The 4♡ bid clearly shows the ♡A, and a liking for clubs. That is all East needs to know. If a small slam with 13 points opposite a weak no trump shocks you, reflect on the fact that all thirteen tricks will be made if the ♣Q comes down!

♠ AQJ1087		♠ K95	West	East
♡ A4	N	♡ KQ107	2♠	3♠
◇ 75	W E	◇ AJ103	4♣	4◇
♣ AK4	S	♣ 85	4♡	5♡
			6♣	7♠

Having agreed the trump suit East/West set out on a cuebidding sequence. 4♣, 4◇ and 4♡ are all first-round controls. Now 5♡ and 6♣ (this last bid guarantees a small slam and shows interest in the grand) are second-round controls. At this point East is fairly sure he can count thirteen tricks so he bids the grand slam.

	♠ AJ986		North	South
	♡ A875		Pass	1◇
	◇ 9742		2♠(i)	3♣(ii)
	♣ –		3♡(ii)	4♡(iii)
♠ Q32		♠ K1074	4♠(ii)	5♡(iii)
♡ J943	N	♡ 102	6♣(iv)	7◇(v)
◇ 8	W E	◇ Q5		
♣ KQ1086	S	♣ J9532		
	♠ 5			
	♡ KQ6			
	◇ AKJ1063			
	♣ A74			

(i) The jump bid after passing is universally recognised in good circles as natural but with partner's suit – in this case diamonds. Without a fit you don't jump.

(ii) Cuebids showing first-round control.

(iii) Cuebid showing second- and third-round control of hearts.

(iv) Actually a first-round control but North has only now been able to get the information across.

(v) Everything seems to be wrapped up so let's go for the jackpot.

As you can see, the grand slam is virtually lay-down, but the bidding... that was quite something.

My final hand almost ended in disaster as North/South stretched themselves to the limit – and perhaps a bit beyond!

East/West Game. IMPs. Dealer North

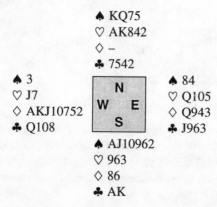

	♠ KQ75	
	♡ AK842	
	◇ –	
	♣ 7542	
♠ 3		♠ 84
♡ J7	N	♡ Q105
◇ AKJ10752	W E	◇ Q943
♣ Q108	S	♣ J963
	♠ AJ10962	
	♡ 963	
	◇ 86	
	♣ AK	

West	North	East	South
–	1♡	Pass	1♠
2♢	3♠	Pass	4♣
Pass	4♢	Pass	5♣
Pass	5♡	Pass	6♣
Pass	6♡	Pass	7♠

Once spades were agreed South cuebid his club controls while North showed first-round controls in diamonds and hearts. No doubt South hoped his partner held the ♡Q instead of the ♠Q, however, it does seem to me that South was rather optimistic (three small cards in partner's suit is not ideal) but, in fact, he made his contract. Can you?

It won't come as a surprise to know that the grand slam was not bid in the other room. However, it is no good criticising South too much, as his card play easily justified his bidding. The ♢A was led and ruffed in dummy. At first sight, prospects did not look good, as it appeared that declarer must lose a trick in hearts. However, two rounds of spades were followed by the ♣A and a second diamond ruff. Declarer returned to hand with the ♣K and continued playing spades to reach the following position:

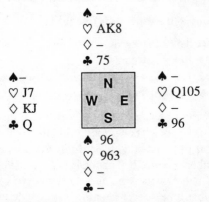

When the ♠9 was played West discarded a diamond and dummy the ♡8, but East was not a happy man. If he discarded a heart, the ♡AK would leave the South hand high; while, if he discarded a club, declarer had only to ruff one club to make the dummy high.

It is true to say that cuebids alone cannot take all the credit for the happy outcome on this hand. A little luck and skilful declarer play certainly helped. Still, without the use of cuebids, there must be some doubt about arriving in the small slam, let alone the ambitious grand. Long live cuebids!

Roman Key Card Blackwood

Star Rating: ✳✳✳✳

Most bridge players are reared on a few simple conventions and it would be a fair bet to assume that one of these is Blackwood, perhaps the easiest and most popular convention in the world. Conceived by the American Master, Easley Blackwood of Indianapolis, as long ago as 1933 and, like Johnnie Walker, is still going strong. It is remarkable that his original idea has required little doctoring over the passing years. Perhaps the most significant improvement was to count the king of trumps as a fifth 'ace' and amend the responses to incorporate this feature. However, once it is intended to break away from the basic traditional form of Blackwood, which incidentally is still played in most rubber-bridge circles, perhaps we should go the whole hog and examine the most streamlined and popular concept of modern Blackwood. This is Roman Key Card Blackwood.

RKCB recognises the vital role played by the king and queen of trumps and this is reflected in the schedule of responses to 4NT. Initially the responses are geared to the four aces and the king of trumps, thus there are five key cards involved (the queen of trumps enters the stage later on, as an accessory).

These are the responses to partner's 4NT enquiry:

5♣ 0 or 3 key cards
5◇ 1 or 4 key cards
5♡ 2 or 5 key cards without the trump queen
5♠ 2 or 5 key cards with the trump queen

If you think there might be some ambiguity over the dual role that these responses embrace – forget it! The previous bidding will always make the situation clear, but if by some odd quirk of fate you are uncertain, assume partner has the weaker version. If it happens to be the stronger one he will continue bidding when next it is his turn to speak. To comfort you, perhaps I should add that it has never been my experience to witness a competent pair have a misunderstanding in this particular area.

As with all forms of slam investigation, it is necessary to have first agreed on a satisfactory trump suit, and then to make sure that partner's reply to your 4NT enquiry will not prove an embarrassment. If it might, then maybe you should curb your enthusiasm and proceed in a different way.

Over the responses of 5♣ and 5◇ (4NT–5♣/5◇) you can check on the trump queen by bidding the next suit up – excluding the trump suit. If the responder does not hold the trump queen he must sign off in the agreed trump suit, holding the trump queen he may cuebid an outside king or bid 5NT.

After using 4NT you may then ask for kings (excluding the trump king, of course) by bidding 5NT. This reply should be based on the ladder principle as used in basic Blackwood, i.e. 6♣ = 0, 6◇ = 1, etc. But please note that the bid of 5NT guarantees that all five key cards are held by the partnership.

What happens when the responder to 4NT has a useful void i.e. not a void in partner's suit? There are a number of different ideas but I suggest the following: Make the same bid as you would normally but now make it at the six level providing that this bid is not higher than the agreed trrump suit, otherwise respond six of the agreed trump suit. Obviously some discretion is required in this area.

Let us look at an example.

	♠ K8			♠ A642
	♡ QJ108	**N**		♡ AK9642
	◇ 102	**W E**		◇ –
	♣ AKQ106	**S**		♣ 942

West	North	East	South
1♣	1◇	1♡	2◇
3♡	Pass	3♠(i)	Pass
4♣(i)	Pass	4◇(i)	Pass
4NT(ii)	Pass	6♣(iii)	Pass
7♡(iv)	All Pass		

(i)   Cuebids.
(ii) RKCB.
(iii) 0 or 3 keycards (it can't be nil), plus a useful void.
(iv) The grand slam must surely be icy.

In general terms, if two key cards are missing you should sign off at the five level. If only one key card is missing, a small slam should be worth bidding. If there are no key cards missing then a grand slam could be the answer but you may still want to check up on the queen of trumps or a side suit king. You now have the machinery, so let's see it in operation:

♠ AJ964			♠ KQ83	**West**	**East**
♡ AQ5	**N**		♡ K92	1♠	4♠
◇ KQ83	**W E**		◇ 74	4NT(i)	5♠(ii)
♣ 6	**S**		♣ AJ82	6♠(iii)	

After a natural opening bid and response West senses that there may well
be a slam. The 4NT (i) RKCB enquiry reveals a great deal of information.
5♠ (ii) says I have two key cards, plus the queen of trumps. West now
knows that one key-card is missing but decides the small slam (iii) should
be a good bet. It is:

♠ A8		♠ K63	**West**	**East**
♡ KQ84	N	♡ AJ1073	1♣	1♡
◇ K3	W E	◇ A64	3♡	4NT(i)
♣ A9864	S	♣ K7	5♣(ii)	5◇(iii)
			6◇(iv)	7♡(v)

The promising start encourages East to trot out his toy, RKCB (i),
although it wouldn't have been wrong to have exchanged a couple of cuebids first (4◇-4♠). Notice how the reply, 5♣ (ii) simply cannot be
ambiguous. Nil or three key cards. Yes, of course it has to be *three*,
immediately identifiable as the black-suit aces and the king of hearts. 5◇
(iii) asks for the queen of trumps. West has got it (iv) (without it he would
have to sign off in 5♡) so he shows the ◇K as well. He could also reply
5NT (yes, I have the trump queen and a side-suit king too) if a response at
the six level looked dangerous (the ♠K, for example). Perhaps East cannot immediately underwrite the grand slam (v) but it certainly looks a
good odds-on chance. In practice it was Momma-Poppa.

♠ KJ82		♠ AQ964	**West**	**East**
♡ 75	N	♡ K3	1◇	1♠
◇ AKJ32	W E	◇ Q10	2♠	3♣(i)
♣ 86	S	♣ A542	4♠(ii)	4NT(iii)
			5♡(iv)	6♠(v)

When West raised to 2♠, East thought he would try and glean a little
more information. 3♣ (i) looked like a trial bid for game to West who
responded positively by jumping to 4♠(ii). East was now sufficiently
encouraged to try 4NT (iii), RKCB. 5♡ (iv) showed two key-cards and,
of course, denied the queen of trumps. East decided to risk the slam (v)
and as soon as he saw dummy he was glad he had done so.

Roman Key Card Blackwood has a lot going for it. A few more i's get
dotted and a few more t's get crossed. In a sophisticated world where tech-
nology is always advancing even Blackwood can become more streamlined, more vibrant.

5NT Grand Slam Asking Bid

Star Rating: ✲✲✲✲✲

The original 5NT asking bid, often referred to economically as Josephine (named after Josephine Culbertson the originator) was simplicity itself. It asked a straightforward question and received an uncomplicated answer.

The 5NT Question: have you two of the top three honours (AKQ) in our agreed trump suit?

The Reply: With two of the three, bid seven in the agreed trump suit. With only one, or fewer, bid six in the agreed trump suit.

Here is an example from yesteryear.

♠ KQ85		♠ AJ764	**West**	**East**
♡ QJ1074	N	♡ AK	1♡	2♠
◇ AJ8	W E	◇ K52	3♠	4♣
♣ 6	S	♣ A93	4◇	5NT
			7♠	

Using cuebids to check that there were no outside losers, East then jumped to 5NT to find out about the K♠ and Q♠. West had them both so bid the grand slam. Missing one of these honours he would have replied 6♠ which would have become the final contract.

Note: The 5NT Grand Slam Force (GSF) can only be used when it is not preceded by 4NT (4NT followed by 5NT is Blackwood asking for kings). The GSF should not be used until it is ascertained that there are no outside losers.

In most rubber-bridge circles this method is still used today. However, it is not accurate enough for most progressive partnerships and, indeed, there is plenty of room for improvement. When one considers spreading the net it is sensible to adopt a system which is efficient yet does not test the memory too severely – especially as the use of the GSF is not an everyday occurrence.

One invaluable addition is to use the response of 6♣ (to 5NT, the GSF) to indicate Axxxx or Kxxxx in the agreed trump suit. This would bring into the net many nearly 80% or 90% grand slams that would otherwise be impossible to bid with accuracy under traditional methods.

Study the following:

♠ A10	N	♠ K83	**West**	**East**
♡ A10864		♡ K7532	1♡	3♡
◇ AKQ72	W E	◇ 84	3♠(i)	4♣(i)
♣ 4	S	♣ A73	4◇(i)	4♠(ii)
			5NT(iii)	6♣(iv)
			7♡(v)	

(i)   Cuebids, all showing first-round control.

(ii) Second-round control of spades.

(iii) The Grand Slam Trump Asking Bid, or GSF for short.

(iv) This has to be Kxxxx as West has the ace himself.

(v)   West knows that the grand slam is about 78%. Good enough odds to have a go. With the ♡J instead of the ♡10 the odds would improve to about 89%.

To make life as easy and comfortable as possible, we can retain the response of seven to show two of the top three honours, and the response of six to show none where the agreed trump suit is a major, but to show one or none where it is a minor.

In every case, except where clubs is the agreed trump suit, the response of six clubs shows Axxxx or Kxxxx. This is how the responses work.

The replies to 5NT (GSF) when the trump suit is clubs:

   7♣ = Two of the top three honours

   6♣ = One or none of the top three honours

The replies to 5NT (GSF) when the trump suit is diamonds:

   7◇ = Two of the top three honours

   6◇ = One or none of the three top honours

   6♣ = Axxxx or Kxxxx in diamonds

The replies to 5NT (GSF) when the trump suit is hearts:

   7♡ = Two of the top three honours

   6♡ = None of the top three honours

   6◇ = One of the top three honours with a maximum of four
          trumps, or Qxxxx, unless the bidding indicates differently
          (a pre-empt, for example)

   6♣ = Axxxx or Kxxxx in hearts

The replies to 5NT (GSF) when the trump suit is spades:

   7♠ = Two of the top three honours

6♠ = None of the top three honours

6♡ = One of the top three honours with a maximum of four trumps, unless the bidding indicates differently (a pre-empt, for example)

6♢ = Qxxxx in spades

6♣ = Axxxx or Kxxxx in spades

With a little more room to move when the agreed trump suit is a major we can get some extra information across. This is especially true when spades are going to be trumps as we can now show one of the top three honours with four trumps. Also queen to five and then ace or king to five.

All valuable data which is fairly easily assimilated as the bids of seven and six of the agreed trump suit and 6♣ (except where clubs are going to be trumps) are constant throughout.

Because of the popularity of Roman Key Card Blackwood, which accounts for the AKQ of trumps, Josephine is used much less these days. However, that is not to say that you can dispose of the GSF entirely when you have adopted RKCB. There are moments when you will still have to rely on it. For example, when holding a void the 4NT enquiry is often less than completely satisfactory, and in some cuebidding sequences you may have to pass the 4NT level before you can decide how best to progress.

The following hands illustrate these points.

♠ KQ		♠ A864	West	East
♡ KQ84	N	♡ AJ9753	1♢	1♡
♢ AQ1063	W E	♢ KJ5	4♡	4♠
♣ 105	S	♣ —	5♢	5NT
			7♡	

Over West's rebid of 4♡ it would be foolish for East to bid 4NT because he wouldn't know for sure whether West held the ♢A or the ♣A. The cuebid of 4♠ gets the reply of 5♢ (the ♢A) and now 5NT (GSF) asks about the top three honours. Holding both the king and queen West is only too happy to bid 7♡.

♠ 4		♠ A52
♡ KJ109865	N	♡ AQ4
♢ J7	W E	♢ —
♣ A42	S	♣ KQ108754

West	North	East	South
3♡	3♠	4♠	Pass
5♣	Pass	5NT	Pass
6♢	Pass	7♡	All Pass

4♠ agrees hearts as the trump suit and when West is able to cuebid the ♣A East's only concern is whether he holds the ♡K as well. 5NT asks the question and the reply of 5♢ confirms one of the top three honours. Obviously, in this case the number of cards in the trump suit does not apply because of West's pre-empt.

♠ KQ7		♠ A104	
♡ A974	N	♡ K10865	
♢ 4	W E	♢ A3	
♣ KQJ85	S	♣ A64	

West	North	East	South
1♣	3♢	3♡	5♢
5♡	Pass	5NT	Pass
6♢	Pass	6♡	

From East's point of view 7♡ might be cold if West has both the ♡A and ♡Q. However, the reply to 5NT confirms that this is not the case so East subsides in 6♡.

4

GETTING TO BETTER SLAMS

We saw in the last chapter how cuebidding, Roman Key Card Blackwood and the Grand Slam Force could improve your slam bidding overnight. This chapter features four more conventions commonly in play in tournament bridge which will help you become even more effective. The language of bidding is a very restricted one, and each pair should work hard to increase their understanding. In the finely tuned area of slams the need for accuracy is paramount. Bidding good slams and staying out of bad slams is what it is all about. Here are four more conventional aides.

Swiss

Star Rating: ✳✳✳✳

The Swiss convention consists of a jump to 4♣ or 4◇ by responder to an opening bid of 1♡ or 1♠. The idea is to differentiate between game going hands that are shapely but lack aces (1♡–4♡ or 1♠–4♠), and hands that are rich in aces and therefore may have slam potential.

Suppose your partner opens the bidding with 1♡ and you hold either of the following hands:

(a)	♠ 4	(b)	♠ A83
	♡ K10964		♡ QJ1064
	◇ KQ875		◇ 6
	♣ 63		♣ A874

By all usual methods of valuation you are worth a raise to game. But how is partner to know that on hand (a) you are all shape and hope, while on (b) your controls are eye catching and there is a positive spring in your step?

The Swiss idea (it originated in Switzerland in the first place, hence the name) was to use the response of 4♣ or 4◇ (to one of a major) to indicate the more promising type of hand with an emphasis on controls. A sort of advanced announcement that responder is suitable for slam purposes should that suggestion appeal to opener in any way. The loss of the direct minor suit responses (1♡/1♠–4♣/4◇), on a frequency basis alone, was minimal. After all, how often do you want to respond four of a minor in the natural sense? Certainly not sufficiently to regret discarding it for a far more useful purpose. Using the Swiss convention then, the direct major suit game raise (1♡/1♠–4♡/4♠) denies the qualifications attributed to Swiss.

Although Swiss is played in a number of different ways this is the method I suggest you adopt.

West opens 1♡ or 1♠. East responds 4♣.

The response of 4♣ shows game going values in partner's major, 13-15 points including distributional points, four trumps or more, of course, plus one of the following conditions:

(1) Three aces.
(2) Two aces and a singleton.
(3) Two aces and the king of trumps.

Should opener wish to inquire further he now bids 4◇ over 4♣ and responder continues as follows:

(1) 4NT – three aces.
(2) Bid the suit with the singleton – two aces and a singleton.
(3) Reverts to four of the trump suit – two aces and the king of trumps.

Note: with two aces, a singleton and the king of trumps, responder shows the singleton first.

West opens 1♡ or 1♠. East responds 4◇.

The response of 4◇ also shows game going values in partner's major, 13-15 points including distributional points, four trumps or more and two aces. But this bid denies the other requirements of the 4♣ bid (i.e. no singleton, third ace or trump king). Valuable negative information, perhaps, while still retaining the emphasis on aces.

Let us see Swiss at work:

West	(a) East	(b) East	(c) East
♠ AKJ96	♠ Q1084	♠ Q1084	♠ 10875
♡ J1085	♡ 6	♡ A964	♡ A6
◇ KQ	◇ A1075	◇ 5	◇ AJ75
♣ K4	♣ AQ83	♣ AQJ3	♣ A83

West opens 1♠ and in each case East responds 4♣. So East has either two aces and a singleton or three aces. The third qualification – two aces and the king of trumps – is negated by West's own trump holding. West continues with 4◇ – clarification please. On hand (a) East replies 4♡. That is exactly what West wanted to hear – a singleton heart – and so he bids a confident 6♠. On (b) East replies 5◇. That is bad news. A singleton diamond opposite the bare KQ does nothing for West's slam prospects so he signs off in 5♠. On (c) East replies 4NT – three aces – so there is no clear cut answer. There might be two heart losers, or one heart and one spade, or perhaps just one heart. West might try a cuebid of 5♣ hoping that East could show a doubleton or some other feature but obviously East's options will be limited. In the actual example East would continue with 5♡ leaving West the final decision. If West's spades were headed by the AKQ, instead of the AKJ, then he would be able to bid the slam with confidence.

The following hands are worth further study:

♠ K75		♠ A83	**West**	**East**
♡ AK1082	**N**	♡ QJ964	1♡	4♣
◇ A974	**W E**	◇ 6	4◇	5◇
♣ 5	**S**	♣ A874	6♡	

With only 14 HCPs, West has no qualms about bidding the slam.

♠ 6		♠ AJ84	**West**	**East**
♡ AQJ973	**N**	♡ K1086	1♡	4♣
◇ K10	**W E**	◇ AJ74	4◇	5♣
♣ A842	**S**	♣ 5	5♠	7♡

After a promising start West inquires with 4◇ and East shows a singleton club. West can virtually count twelve tricks so he now makes a grand slam try with 5♠. East realises that the king of trumps must be the card his partner wants for thirteen tricks, so he bids a confident 7♡.

Suppose in response to the same hand East held only three spades and a doubleton club so that the two hands looked like this:

♠ 6		♠ AJ4	**West**	**East**
♡ AQJ973	**N**	♡ K1086	1♡	4♣
◇ K10	**W E**	◇ AJ74	4◇	4♡
♣ A842	**S**	♣ 75	6♡	

Now there would be no temptation for West to proceed beyond 6♡.

Here is another example of complete trust after the initial, more or less automatic, exchanges have been made.

		West	East
♠ AQ9865	♠ KJ103	**West**	**East**
♡ AKQ	♡ 862	1♠	4♣
◇ 754	◇ A	4◇	5◇
♣ 3	♣ A9743	5♡	6♠
		7♠	

The bids up to 5◇ are routine, East showing two aces and a singleton diamond which, of course, has to be the ace. West then makes a cuebid of 5♡. With the king of trumps not yet accounted for East jumps to 6♠. West interprets this development correctly and bids the lay down grand slam.

The response of 4◇ (1♡/1♠–4◇), while encouraging in one sense (two aces), offers a salutary warning against expecting too much:

		West	East
♠ Q63	♠ AJ10	**West**	**East**
♡ AQJ86	♡ 10975	1♡	4◇
◇ KQJ	◇ 73	4♡	
♣ 105	♣ AKJ6		

Knowing that one ace and the ♡K are missing West is not tempted to be ambitious.

		West	East
♠ AQ74	♠ K5	**West**	**East**
♡ AK1084	♡ Q975	1♡	4◇
◇ K6	◇ A853	4NT(i)	5◇(ii)
♣ 83	♣ A64	6♡	

(i) How many kings?
(ii) One

West's bid of 4NT asks for *kings* – aces are already known – and when East shows one king the small slam looks a reasonable proposition.

Of course, there will be many occasions when the opener will not want to make further enquiries after the bidding has started 1♡/1♠–4♣.

♠ 74
♡ A9864
◇ AK5
♣ Q63

West opens 1♡ and hears 4♣ from his partner. Having no further ambitions he will sign off in 4♡.

It is important to remember that the 4♣, or 4◇, response to 1♡ or 1♠ should be limited in that it does not contain forcing values. 13-15 points, including distribution, is about right. Suppose you hold ♠AK1093 ♡KQ72 ◇8 ♣A83 and hear partner bid 1♡ – what is your response? With 16 HCPs plus two distributional points for the singleton diamond you are much too strong for Swiss. Your best bid is 2♠, a game force.

Splinter Bids

Star Rating: ✳✳✳✳

A Splinter Bid is an unusual jump in a new suit which guarantees a fit for partner's last named suit (at least four card support) and shows a singleton or void in the suit in which the jump is made. Game is confirmed and a slam is suggested if partner is suitable.

You will notice that there is some similarity between Splinter Bids and Swiss in that the objectives, and to some extent the qualifications, occupy common ground. The main difference is that Swiss is primarily harnessed to aces, while Splinter Bids are concerned with singletons (the singleton may be an ace) and voids. The last bid in each of the following is a Splinter:

> (a) 1♡–3♠
> (b) 1♣–1♡–4◇
> (c) 1♠–2◇–4♣
> (d) 1♠–2♣–2♡–4◇
> (e) 1♠–4♡ (be sure that your partner is on the same
>   wavelength as you for this one)
> (f) 1♠–4♣
> (g) 1♡–4◇

If you play Swiss you might, like me, prefer to reserve (f) and (g) for the Swiss convention only. If you don't play Swiss then these sequences, 1♡/1♠–4♣/4◇, fall neatly into the Splinter Bid category.

In general, any jump during the auction when a lower level bid, or lower level jump bid, would be forcing, should be considered a Splinter Bid. A repeat bid in the Splinter suit confirms either the singleton ace or a void. Otherwise new suits are cuebids while 4NT is Blackwood.

How strong should you be to initiate a Splinter Bid?

If you are responder you require at least four card support for partner's suit (usually a major) and the equivalent of a minimum opening bid, about 13-15 points including distributional points, or six or seven losers. If you have more points or only five losers you will probably be too strong for a Splinter and should be considering a jump bid in a new suit. Let's look at some examples. Partner opens 1♡ and you hold:

(a) ♠ KQ1064	(b) ♠964
♡ AQ105	♡ KJ1053
◊ 4	◊ 4
♣ J97	♣ A642
Bid 4◊	Bid 3♡

(c) ♠ A76	(d) ♠ 6
♡ KQ105	♡ KQ105
◊ 4	◊ AQ109
♣ AKJ104	♣ J1064
Bid 3♣	Bid 3♠

(a) and (d) are natural Splinter hands. (b) is too weak for a splinter so you just make the normal limit raise to 3♡. (c) is too strong for a Splinter Bid. It is best to force at once.

If you are the opener and strong enough to jump to game in responder's suit (1◊–1♡–4♡), i.e. you hold 19+ points and no more than five losers, you should prefer a Splinter Bid whenever that is available. You open 1◊ and your partner responds 1♡. You hold:

(a) ♠ KQ6	(b) ♠ 8
♡ AQ105	♡ KQ75
◊ AKJ104	◊ AKQ105
♣ –	♣ A43
Bid 4♣	Bid 3♠

(c) ♠ AJ9	(d) ♠ A
♡ QJ84	♡ KQ92
◊ AKJ973	◊ KQJ105
♣ –	♣ Q105
Bid 4♣	Bid 3♠

Object of Splinter Bids

The idea is to explore for slam, trying to discover if there is perhaps a super fit which sometimes will enable it to be bid on quite minimum high cards. Equally important is the other side of the coin – Splinter Bids may help you to stay out of a poor slam that might otherwise be bid on general values. Let's look at the system at work.

Game All. IMPs. Dealer West.

```
♠ QJ5              ♠ A4
♡ AQ96            ♡ KJ1075
◇ AKQ104         ◇ 853
♣ 7               ♣ 964
```

In the open room the bidding was of a fairly pedestrian nature. West opened 1◇, East responded 1♡ and West raised to 4♡, where the matter rested.

In the closed room, after a similar start, 1◇–1♡, West rebid 4♣–a Splinter Bid agreeing hearts and showing a singleton or void club. East gave his next bid a little thought. Having no wastage in clubs was good news, but three little cards in partner's first suit is always an unattractive holding when considering slam and East was well aware of the dangers. On the other hand, he did have good trumps and an ace. In any case a cue-bid would not necessarily commit him to slam so he ventured 4♠. This was all West wanted to hear and he bid a confident 6♡.

Although South held some promising cards on the next deal, he heeded the gipsy's warning when North's rebid started the alarm bells ringing.

Love All. Pairs. Dealer North.

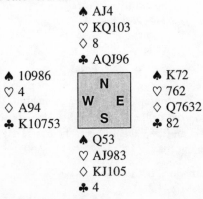

```
                  ♠ AJ4
                  ♡ KQ103
                  ◇ 8
                  ♣ AQJ96
♠ 10986                        ♠ K72
♡ 4                            ♡ 762
◇ A94                          ◇ Q7632
♣ K10753                       ♣ 82
                  ♠ Q53
                  ♡ AJ983
                  ◇ KJ105
                  ♣ 4
```

North opened 1♣ and then rebid 4◇ over 1♡. Tempting though it was, South decided that the hands were too ill-fitting to go slamming and shut up shop with a bid of 4♡. This turned out to be a wise decision because a spade was led and there was no way he could make more than eleven tricks. Plus 450 on the score sheet was a pleasing sight.

The next hand was played in a Swiss Teams event. One North counted his points and allowed them to control his destiny.

The other North – well let's see.

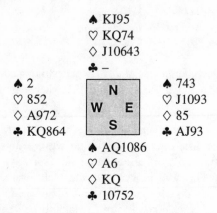

♠ KJ95
♡ KQ74
◇ J10643
♣ –

♠ 2   ♠ 743
♡ 852   ♡ J1093
◇ A972   ◇ 85
♣ KQ864   ♣ AJ93

♠ AQ1086
♡ A6
◇ KQ
♣ 10752

At the first table the bidding was 1♠–4♠ and North thought he had been very forward in bidding 4♠, not 3♠ – 'Only 10 points, partner'.

At the opposite table this was the auction:

South	North
1♠	4♣
4♡	5♣
5◇	5♡
6♠	Pass

4♣ was a splinter agreeing spades. 4♡ was a cuebid, denying the ◇A, and 5♣ confirmed a void or the singleton ♣A. 5◇ showed second round control in diamonds and 5♡ the same in hearts. That was enough for South to bid a confident 6♠.

Twelve tricks were made at both tables.

DOPI

Star Rating: ✳✳

You have got together with your partner and agreed a suit while your opponents have been active in the bidding, and then your partner pops the question via Blackwood 4NT, 'How many aces have you?' Nothing too demanding so far but then it happens – your RHO bids one more of his wretched suit and you are suddenly confronted with a problem. How are you to tell partner what he wants to know when the opposition have taken up your space? If you were riding a race you could almost certainly lodge an objection. No doubt there would be a Stewards' Enquiry and justice would prevail. In bridge, however, your opponents are completely within their rights to impede you, take your ground and do their very best to ensure that at all times you get anything but a clear run. To counter this impertinent intrusion into the nice conversation you were having with your partner you need a smidgen of sophistication. Not a lot, but just enough to swing the pendulum back in your favour. Although there are a number of different methods available by far the simplest and most popular is DOPI.

DOPI works like this (remember, over your partner's 4NT bid RHO has come in with, say, 5♡):

With no ace:	Double. That is the DO (Double = 0)
With one ace:	Pass. That is the PI (Pass = 1)
With two aces:	Bid the next suit up. If you've remembered the first bit this and the last case follow along logically.
With three aces:	Bid two suits up.

Thinking about all that for a moment, the worst type of hand you can have for partner for slam purposes is some aceless wonder, so double seems eminently sensible anyway. With one ace that may be good news or bad news, but by passing you will keep partner fully informed and then he can make his own arrangements. With two or three aces that must be good news, so you can afford to get busy.

Let's look at a few sequences to make sure we've got the system taped. You are West.

1.	♠ AQJ96	West	North	East	South
	♡ 75	1♠	2♡	3♡	4♡
	◇ KQ63	Pass	Pass	4NT	5♡
	♣ Q6	?			

Pass, this shows one ace.

2.

	♠ KQ1095	West	North	East	South
	♡ 2	1♠	2♡	3◇	3♡
	◇ KJ96	4◇	Pass	4NT	5♡
	♣ KJ10	?			

Double, this denies an ace.

3.

	♠ AQ1097	West	North	East	South
	♡ 63	–	–	–	1♡
	◇ AQ42	1♠	4♡	4NT	5♡
	♣ 64	?			

Bid 5♠ showing two aces.

4.

	♠ 2	West	North	East	South
	♡ A10963	1♡	1♠	3◇	3♠
	◇ A53	Pass	4♠	4NT	5♠
	♣ AJ85	?			

Bid 6♣ showing three aces. 5NT would show two aces.

Let us look at two of the hands in more depth. On Hand 2, DOPI helped East/West to judge correctly at the five level.

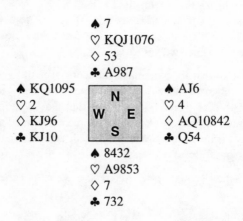

```
                    ♠ 7
                    ♡ KQJ1076
                    ◇ 53
                    ♣ A987
    ♠ KQ1095                      ♠ AJ6
    ♡ 2            N              ♡ 4
    ◇ KJ96      W     E           ◇ AQ10842
    ♣ KJ10         S              ♣ Q54
                    ♠ 8432
                    ♡ A9853
                    ◇ 7
                    ♣ 732
```

West	North	East	South
1♠	2♡	3◇	3♡
4◇	4♡	4NT	5♡
Double	Pass	5♠	All Pass

Warned that there were two aces missing (West's double denies an ace), East's only decision was whether to take a penalty or play in 5♠. In settling for the spade game he judged it right as 5♡ goes only two down whereas West had no difficulty in landing eleven tricks.

On Hand 3, DOPI was used in bidding a good slam.

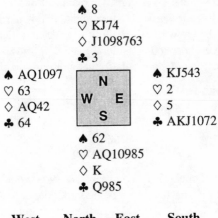

```
                    ♠ 8
                    ♡ KJ74
                    ◇ J1098763
                    ♣ 3
    ♠ AQ1097      ┌─────────┐      ♠ KJ543
    ♡ 63          │    N    │      ♡ 2
    ◇ AQ42        │  W   E  │      ◇ 5
    ♣ 64          │    S    │      ♣ AKJ1072
                  └─────────┘
                    ♠ 62
                    ♡ AQ10985
                    ◇ K
                    ♣ Q985
```

West	North	East	South
–	–	–	1♡
1♠	4♡	4NT	5♡
5♠	Pass	6♠	All Pass

Over the nuisance bid of 5♡, West showed his two aces by bidding one suit up. This was exactly what East wanted to hear and he set course accordingly. The play of the hand presented no problems for West although North/South were not too happy about their decision to defend. 7♡ should cost no more than 1100.

Notice how in each case East/West were not inhibited in any way by the opposition barrage. DOPI solved their problems and left the headaches with North/South.

There are other methods that may be used in this situation. DOPI has the merit of being simple and very effective.

Raises to Five of a Major

Star Rating: ✳✳✳

In an era when bidding was less sophisticated and less meaningful than it is today, free raises to the five level in a major suit were often regarded as being synonymous with an acute attack of buck passing. Bid one more and the slam fails – it's your fault. Chicken out and pass when the slam makes – it's still your fault. A convenient, if not particularly efficient, route for those players who never admit to making a mistake. Fortunately, our methods have improved considerably so that bridge in the '90s is able to clarify the meaning of such bids so that ambiguity is strictly minimised.

Suppose you hold, as West:

♠ –
♡ AK943
♢ 85
♣ AK9762

Your partner, East, opens 1♠. You reply 2♣ (you wouldn't force on a two suited hand, even if you had more points) and, rather to your surprise, you hear partner rebid 2♡. What next? Yes, the correct bid is now 5♡, meaning bid six if you control diamonds. East's hand might be one of the following:

(a) ♠AKJ64	**(b)** ♠ AKJ108	**(c)** ♠ AKJ108	**(d)** ♠ KQ964
♡ QJ875	♡ QJ107	♡ QJ107	♡ QJ107
♢ 7	♢ Q7	♢ A7	♢ K7
♣ 83	♣ QJ	♣ 83	♣ Q3

(a) On this hand 6♡ should be an easy make, and East, following instructions, should bid it:

West	East
–	1♠
2♣	2♡
5♡	6♡
Pass	

(b) On the second hand there is no play for a slam, if a diamond is led, and East should pass:

West	East
–	1♠
2♣	2♡
5♡	Pass

(c) On the third hand East has first round control of the suit his partner is querying, so he bids 6♦, paving the way for a possible grand slam:

West	East
–	1♠
2♣	2♡
5♡	6♦

(d) On the fourth hand East has an aceless minimum, but his partner is not asking him about his overall strength, or the number of aces he holds. He is enquiring solely about diamond control. East has it and should bid 6♡:

West	East
–	1♠
2♣	2♡
5♡	6♡
Pass	

So we can lay down the rules for Case 1.

Case 1

When three suits have been bid and partner goes freely to five of the agreed major – bid six if you control the unbid suit (i.e. not two losers), or cuebid the suit if you have first round control in it.

Let us look at another example. This time West bids first and might hold any of the three following hands:

(a) ♠ KJ86	(b) ♠ KJ86	(c) ♠ KJ86
♡ 53	♡ 53	♡ 53
◇ AKQ97	◇ AKJ973	◇ AK1073
♣ Q6	♣ 6	♣ A6

Opposite East holds:

♠ AQ95	West	East
♡ AK108642	1◇	1♡
◇ –	1♠	5♠
♣ 103	?	

(a) West cannot control the club suit, so should pass 5♠.

(b) With a singleton club, West must bid the slam – 6♠.

(c) With the ♣A, West should bid 6♣. This may lead to a grand slam.

Case 2

When the opponents bid a suit and then you or your partner bid freely to five of your agreed major – bid six if you control their suit

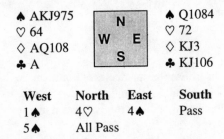

♠ AKJ975		♠ Q1084
♡ 64		♡ 72
◇ AQ108		◇ KJ3
♣ A		♣ KJ106

West	North	East	South
1♠	4♡	4♠	Pass
5♠	All Pass		

Although East/West have tricks to spare in the minors and in the trump suit, they cannot get away from two losing hearts. However, West's message is completely unequivocal, and East has no option but to pass 5♠. With a singleton heart he would, of course, bid the slam.

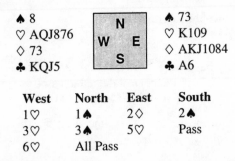

♠ 8		♠ 73
♡ AQJ876		♡ K109
◇ 73		◇ AKJ1084
♣ KQJ5		♣ A6

West	North	East	South
1♡	1♠	2◇	2♠
3♡	3♠	5♡	Pass
6♡	All Pass		

In this example East asks the question 'Do you control the enemy suit?' West does, so he bids the slam.

The last case is when you are looking for 'good' trumps in partner's hand. That is to say 'good' in relation to the bidding. Suppose you open 1♠ as West, partner raises to 4♠, and you hold:

♠ Q9875
♡ AKJ82
◇ A5
♣ A

Now for slam purposes, it seems likely that everything will hinge on the quality of East's spades. For example, East could easily hold any of the following hands:

(a) ♠ J10642	**(b)** ♠ KJ642	**(c)** ♠ AJ106
♡ 7	♡ 7	♡ Q75
◇ KQ843	◇ KJ843	◇ 83
♣ K6	♣ 65	♣ KQ86

To find out about the trumps, West continues by bidding 5♠ (1♠–4♠–5♠). On (a) East will pass, but on (b) and (c) he will continue to 6♠. So these are the rules for Case 3:

Case 3

When only one major suit has been bid against silent opposition, a continuation to the five level asks about the quality of partner's trumps. If good in relation to the bidding, go to six, if not pass.

A common situation arises after an opening bid of 1NT. West opens 1NT (12-14) and East holds:

	West	**East**
♠ Q10864	1NT	3♠
♡ A7	4♠	5♠
◇ AJ10	?	
♣ AKJ		

West could hold any of these hands:

(a) ♠ J975	**(b)** ♠ K52	**(c)** ♠ AK5	**(d)** ♠ AJ95
♡ KQJ	♡ KQ105	♡ K105	♡ KQ10
◇ KQ9	◇ K9	◇ K962	◇ K962
♣ Q108	♣ Q1086	♣ 1086	♣ 106

On (a) West should pass 5♠, but on (c) and (d) he should convert to 6♠. Hand (b) is more debatable, which only goes to prove that there will never be an automatic answer *all the time*. Nevertheless, my feeling is that West should pass. On the given layout, that is likely to be the right decision, as indeed it might be most of the time.

Now let us consider this sequence:

West	**East**
1NT	3♠
4♣	5♠

In effect the only suit bid is spades, because West's rebid of 4♣ agrees spades and shows the ♣A on the way for no extra cost. West might hold any of the following hands:

    (a) ♠ KJ96   (b) ♠ J96   (c) ♠ KJ6
          ♡ Q63   ♡ J5   ♡ AJ106
          ◊ A64   ◊ AK103   ◊ 964
          ♣ A104   ♣ A1042   ♣ A94

On (a) and (c) West should be happy to continue to the slam but on (b) he should pass 5♠.

Now let's look at some hands from competition.

Suppose that, playing in a teams competition, you hold the following hand as East, vulnerable against not.

                  ♠ AQ9632
                  ♡ 84
                  ◊ AK2
                  ♣ A4

You open the bidding with 1♠, South comes in with 4♡ and West bids 4♠ which is passed to you. Would you bid any more? If you did go on, what would you say?

At one table East tried 5♣ but then passed when his partner converted to 5♠. At the opposite table, East tried the effect of a raise to 5♠ and although his partner was clearly reluctant to increase the commitment, discipline won the day and he did bid 6♠. These were the two hands:

     ♠ K1075   ♠ AQ9632
     ♡ 10   N   ♡ 84
     ◊ J983   W   E   ◊ AK2
     ♣ KJ62   S   ♣ A4

At least East/West proved that they were on the same wavelength although perhaps the final contract was no thing of great beauty. The ♡A was led followed by the king which was ruffed in dummy. Superficially it seemed that success would depend on the ◊Q falling in two rounds or the ♣Q being with South.

Anyway trumps were drawn in two rounds and then the ◊AK brought only small cards from the defenders. This was the moment of truth. After a small trance declarer decided to abandon the soft option of the club finesse and go for the minor suit squeeze. After all North was marked with length in the minors so clearly the squeeze was the better mathematical chance.

This was the three card ending.

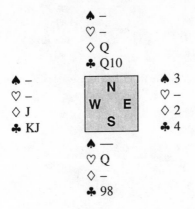

```
              ♠ –
              ♡ –
              ◇ Q
              ♣ Q10
    ♠ –                    ♠ 3
    ♡ –       ┌─────┐      ♡ –
    ◇ J       │  N  │      ◇ 2
    ♣ KJ      │W   E│      ♣ 4
              │  S  │
              └─────┘
              ♠ —
              ♡ Q
              ◇ –
              ♣ 98
```

On the ♠3, South discarded the ♡Q, trying hard to look like a player who was hanging on to the guarded ♣Q. Dummy parted with the ◇J and North did his best by playing the ♣10 smoothly. But East was not to be denied his moment of glory – he played a club to the king and it was all over.

My next example hand occurred in the Women's section of the 1989 European Championships, Great Britain v Netherlands.

South deals at game all, and West holds:

```
              ♠ –
              ♡ J7643
              ◇ A753
              ♣ AKQJ
```

There is no opposition bidding and West opens 1♡ which East raises to 3♡. How should West proceed?

With the opposition remaining ominously silent, there must be some fear that East has wasted honours in spades. Length in spades won't matter, but high cards might if that means that East's trumps are somewhat anaemic at the top. Still, the jump to 5♡, asking for the quality of East's trumps, has much to commend it and, as it happens, would have struck gold. In fact West decided on a cuebid of 5♣. East signed off in 5♡, which became the final contract.

Here are the East/West hands:

♠ –	**N**	♠ 8532
♡ J7643	**W E**	♡ AQ105
◇ A753	**S**	◇ K108
♣ AKQJ		♣ 73

As the ♡K was held by North, all thirteen tricks rolled in without the slightest difficulty.

5
BALANCED HAND BIDDING

Stayman

Star Rating: ✳✳✳✳✳

Stayman, a conventional gadget used to locate a major suit fit (usually 4-4), after a 1NT or 2NT opening, is named after the famous American player Sam Stayman.

Opener bids 1NT (12-14)
When responder wants to ask 'Have you a four card major?' the question is posed by bidding 2♣ (1NT–2♣).

Opener has three possible replies:
    2◊ – No four card major.
    2♡ – Four hearts, may also have four spades.
    2♠ – Four spades. Denies four hearts.

Possible action by responder on receipt of opener's reply:
1. He can sign off in two of his five card major – In order to follow this route responder ought to be at least 5-4 in the majors.
2. He can sign off in 3♣. This will usually be a six card club suit and insufficient values to be interested in game.
3. He can pass if a fit has been found.
4. He can invite game (so his bid is not forcing) with 2NT, 3♡ or 3♠.
5. He can bid game in the agreed suit or raise to 3NT.

These are the holdings when responder can enquire with Stayman:
1. With game going values and at least one four card major, 13+ points.
2. With values to raise to 2NT and at least one four card major, 11-12 points.
3. With a five card major but not enough points to insist on game, perhaps with a 5-4-3-1 shape, 11 points.

4. With five-four in the majors, 0+ points.
5. With a 4-4-5-0 shape, 0+ points.

In all five cases responder can cope with *any* reply by opener to his 2♣ enquiry. This is the essential test when considering the use of Stayman. If the reply to No. 4 is 2◊, responder signs off in two of his five card suit, and if the same reply is made in No 5, responder passes.

The opening bid is 1NT (12-14)
Consider what responder should bid holding:

(a)	♠ AJ96	(b)	♠ 83	(c)	♠ J6
	♡ K1075		♡ AQ75		♡ AK75
	◊ AJ6		◊ KQ754		◊ K1084
	♣ 84		♣ K4		♣ 1075
	2♣		2♣		2♣

(d)	♠ Q853	(e)	♠ 73
	♡ AJ95		♡ 4
	◊ 83		◊ J1098
	♣ J75		♣ K109863
	Pass		2♣

(a) and (b) may play better in a major suit game if a 4-4 fit can be found. Failing that, responder will settle for 3NT. (c) Responder will raise 2♡ to 3♡ or bid 2NT over anything else (invitational, just as though the bidding had gone 1NT–2NT). (d) Responder cannot cope with a response of 2◊, so he must pass. (e) The intention here is to bid 3♣ (sign off) over any response.

(f)	♠ J953	(g)	♠ 109753	(h)	♠ 10842
	♡ KJ965		♡ 8642		♡ A863
	◊ 754		◊ 3		◊ J10754
	♣ 2		♣ 1052		♣ –
	2♣		2♣		2♣

(i)	♠ 97543	(j)	♠ 83
	♡ 108432		♡ AQ1074
	◊ 863		◊ KQ10
	♣ –		♣ A63
	2♣		3♡

Because the shape allows responder to deal with any reply by opener, 2♣ is best in every case except (j). If a fit is not found the responder signs off, 2♡ with (f), and 2♠ with (g). With (h) he passes any reply and with (i) has a choice between 2♡ and 2♠. On (j) there is no point in *asking* about four card majors; better to bid naturally, *showing* the five card major.

Let's see the convention at work.

Opener		Responder	Opener	Responder
♠ Q93		♠ AJ10	1NT	2♣
♡ A1086	N	♡ KQ95	2♡	4♡
◊ A6	W E	◊ 107		
♣ QJ105	S	♣ K963		

3NT would fail on a diamond lead, but Stayman steers the bidding to 4♡.

Opener		Responder	Opener	Responder
♠ AJ96		♠ KQ83	1NT	2♣
♡ KJ84	N	♡ A5	2♡	3NT
◊ Q6	W E	◊ KJ1075	4♠	
♣ Q105	S	♣ 72		

When responder makes it clear that it is not the heart suit that interests him, he must have spades. Opener duly converts 3NT to 4♠ – the best spot.

Opener		Responder	Opener	Responder
♠ Q106		♠ 8	1NT	2♣
♡ A95	N	♡ KJ1064	2◊	3♡
◊ K83	W E	◊ AQ75	4♡	
♣ A1094	S	♣ J75		

Responder's bid of 3♡ (after 2♣, Stayman) is non-forcing but as opener seems to have suitable cards he continues to game.

Stayman works just as efficiently over 2NT. The asking bid, 'Have you a four card major?' is posed by responding 3♣ (2NT–3♣). Opener replies as for 1NT but, of course, at one level higher.

Opener		Responder	Opener	Responder
♠ A103		♠ K753	2NT	3♣
♡ AK83	N	♡ Q1052	3♡	4♡
◊ KQJ7	W E	◊ 1063		
♣ A6	S	♣ J5		

3NT would be hazardous with the club weakness, but 4♡ is sound.

Stayman still applies after a 2♣ opening and 2NT rebid (2♣–2◇–2NT). Here is an example:

Opener		Responder	Opener	Responder
♠ KQ104		♠ J975	2♣	2◇
♡ AK103	N W E S	♡ 84	2NT	3♣
◇ AQJ		◇ K975	3♡	3NT
♣ A8		♣ 643	4♠	

Opener shows a balanced 23-24 points with his 2NT rebid and responder applies Stayman. Hearts is not the suit responder was after so he has to bid 3NT on the third round. However, opener is still there and happily converts to 4♠ knowing that that is where there must be a fit.

Although rather rare, the same machinery can operate when the rebid is 3NT instead of 2NT (2♣–2◇–3NT).

Opener		Responder	Opener	Responder
♠ AKQJ		♠ 9863	2♣	2◇
♡ AJ8	N W E S	♡ Q542	3NT	4♣
◇ KQJ10		◇ 7432	4♠	Pass
♣ KQ		♣ 10		

With two four card majors responder decides to try Stayman, although there is some risk in this sequence. If a fit is not found the final contract will have to be 4NT which might be dangerously high. However, all is well when opener bids 4♠ – the best game contract.

It is worth noting that if the opposition intervene with a bid or a double, Stayman does not apply, e.g.:

West	North	East	South
1NT	2◇	?	

A bid of the opponent's suit (3◇ in this instance) takes the place of Stayman.

West	North	East	South
1NT	Double	2♣	

East's bid of 2♣ is natural, *not* Stayman.

Apart from Blackwood, Stayman is the most universally played convention in the world. You cannot afford to be without it.

Transfers

Star Rating: ✳✳✳✳

Ask any average club player what he understands by Transfers and he will probably reply, 'It enables the strong hand to play the contract.' And, like the curate's egg, that answer is only good in parts. Back in the late fifties, before Transfers had fully developed, the basic idea behind them was indeed to allow the strong hand to become declarer, thus protecting the tenaces and delicate holdings like Kx from the opening lead. (On this basis alone surely everyone should at least play Transfers over 2NT.)

However advantageous it may be for the opening hand to play the contract, the real merit of Transfers lies in the additional information that they can convey. It would be neat and tidy if I could lay down a universal procedure that everyone plays but unfortunately there are a number of variations going the rounds. Anyway, I plan to give you a playable method with as few complexities as possible. So initially let us consider Transfers that you can use after your partner has opened 1NT or 2NT.

Transfer Responses to 1NT (12-14)

2♣ is still your usual Stayman bid.

2♦ is a Transfer to 2♡.

2♡ is a Transfer to 2♠.

2♠ is a Transfer to 2NT if opener is minimum, otherwise he starts bidding his four card suits in ascending order.

2NT is a Transfer to 3♣.

The Response of 2♦ to 1NT

Responder guarantees at least five hearts and requires opener to rebid 2♡. There the contract may rest, just as though you had signed off yourself, or you may continue with a number of informative bids that may invite your partner's further cooperation. Let us consider some hands. Remember, your partner has opened 1NT and you have replied 2♦.

Responder holds:

1.　　♠763　　　　　　　　1NT　　2♦
　　　♡Q10742　　　　　　2♡　　?
　　　♢5
　　　♣A964

Pass. Arranging for partner to play in 2♡ is surely the best you can do so pass his forced rebid.

2.   ♠ AJ3   1NT   2◇
       ♡ Q10742   2♡   ?
       ◇ 53
       ♣ A96

Bid 2NT. This is your normal try for game but in the process you have been able to tell partner that you have five hearts. (Opener will now pass, raise to 3NT or bid 3♡ or 4♡ with three card support or better.)

3.   ♠ AJ3   1NT   2◇
       ♡ KQ1074   2♡   ?
       ◇ 53
       ♣ A96

You are now a little stronger so bid 3NT showing values to go to game plus a five card heart suit. (Opener will either pass, convert to 4♡ or, if especially suitable, cuebid a minor suit ace en route to a heart contract.)

4.   ♠ A6   1NT   2◇
       ♡ AJ9743   2♡   ?
       ◇ J108
       ♣ 53

You are worth a try without insisting. Raise to 3♡. Partner already knows that you have five, so your raise shows six. He should pass or raise to 4♡.

5.   ♠ AK   1NT   2◇
       ♡ A97432   2♡   ?
       ◇ QJ10
       ♣ 53

You must now be in game so bid 4♡. You could have bid this over 1NT, but as you lack tenaces it may be advantageous for partner to play the hand.

6.   ♠ 63   1NT   2◇
       ♡ AK743   2♡   ?
       ◇ A10
       ♣ KQ105

This time anything from 3NT to 6♣ is possible – so bid 3♣. There are various opinions but I would play this bid as forcing to game and how high you get will depend on the subsequent exchange of information, but 3NT from the opener will close the auction.

The Response of 2♡ to 1NT

Responder now guarantees at least five spades and requires opener to bid 2♠. The procedure is then similar to that described already.

The Response of 2♠ to 1NT

The response of 2♠ should ostensibly be reserved for hands strong enough to investigate for slam but without a five card suit. This game forcing bid initiates a sequence in which both players name their four card suits in ascending order until either a fit is found or 3NT is reached.

But note, if opener's 1NT is minimum he must rebid 2NT over 2♠ and then responder starts the action of bidding his four card suits. This proviso allows an important adjunct because responder can also use the 2♠ response on an 11-12 point balanced hand without a four card major. If opener rebids 2NT responder passes. If opener starts bidding his four card suits (so he is maximum) responder shuts up shop with 3NT.

We had better look at some examples.

1. Responder holds:

♠ A7	1NT 2♠
♡ Q103	2NT ?
◊ KQ104	
♣ 9765	

Pass. Partner is minimum. Had partner started bidding his four card suits, responder would have closed the auction with 3NT.

2.

Opener		Responder	Opener	Responder
♠ A4		♠ KQ85	1NT	2♠
♡ QJ4	N	♡ AK6	3♣	3◊
◊ K1075	W E	◊ QJ98	4◊	4♡
♣ K1065	S	♣ A7	4♠	5♣
			6◊	Pass

Responder knows that his partner is maximum (the pluses come from the two tens and the two four card suits) with four clubs and four diamonds. 4♡, 4♠ and 5♣ are all cuebids and 6◊ is the natural outcome. The extra trick by ruffing makes the slam an excellent proposition whereas a no trump contract would have to be fortunate to make more than eleven tricks, Traditional methods via Stayman would uncover a 4-4 major fit but not a minor fit.

3.

Opener	Responder	Opener	Responder
♠ K105	♠ AQ6	1NT	2♠
♡ A863	♡ K7	2NT	3♣
◇ Q8	◇ AK92	4♣	4◇
♣ K1075	♣ A864	4♡	6♣
		Pass	

N
W   E
S

Although opener shows a minimum hand responder is anxious to locate a fit which he finds when opener makes his third bid. The 4♣ bid is worth noting, as with no four card suit other than clubs opener would rebid 3NT over 3♣. With normal breaks 6♣ will succeed while 6NT would be poor.

The Response of 2NT to 1NT

This bid requests partner to bid 3♣ so that responder can sign off in 3♣ or 3◇, indicating at least a six card suit.

Responder holds:

1.

♠ 6	1NT	2NT
♡ A84	3♣	?
◇ 1075		
♣ QJ10974		

Pass. You may or may not make this contract but (a) it is likely to be best, (b) the lead will come up to partner, (c) the 2NT bid has taken away some of the enemy's bidding space.

2.

♠ 74	1NT	2NT
♡ –	3♣	?
◇ KJ109742		
♣ 10874		

Bid 3◇. Traditional methods would allow you to bid 2◇ immediately but it is unlikely that you would be allowed to play there. If you hold the contract in 3◇ you may well feel satisfied whatever the result.

Although responder's 2NT bid (1NT–2NT) ostensibly suggests a weak minor suit with the intention of playing in 3♣ (the forced rebid) or 3◇, there is a further extension which can be invaluable when the right hands come along. Suppose you hold:

♠ KQ10
♡ 5
◇ A107
♣ AQ10764

and hear your partner open 1NT. Without much enthusiasm you respond 2NT and partner dutifully rebids 3♣. You now make the (apparently) strange bid of 3♡. In fact this bid shows a singleton heart plus a long minor (usually six cards). Although partner does not yet know your minor suit the fact that you have been able to indicate your singleton is more than a little encouraging when the two hands are like this:

Responder		Opener	Responder	Opener
♠ KQ10		♠ A963	–	1NT
♡ 5	**N**	♡ J108	2NT	3♣
◊ A107	**W E**	◊ KJ5	3♡	3♠
♣ AQ10764	**S**	♣ KJ3	4♣	4♠
			6♣	Pass

With an unsuitable hand opener would sign off over 3♡ with 3NT, but with little wasted in hearts, and good minors, he is only too happy to cooperate. 3♠ awaits further details, 4♣ names the suit and 4♠ is a cue-bid. Trusting partner for the promised suitable hand, responder bids what he thinks he can make – 6♣. The contract is not lay down, but it is one you would want to be in. Make the opener's hand a fraction more suitable,

♠ AJ63
♡ J108
◊ KJ5
♣ K93

and twelve tricks are virtually guaranteed.

Before we go on to look at Transfers over 2NT, let me make one point clear. If the opposition interfere with a double, Transfers (and Stayman too for that matter) are out. Partner's bid is an attempt to escape into his long suit. This is no time for painting pretty pictures.

Transfer Responses to 2NT (20-22)
All the old arguments now apply with even greater vigour – it is wise to arrange for the strong hand to play the contract and get the lead up to, rather than through, the tenace holdings – but even so the extra dimension in bidding is often invaluable.

3♣ is still Stayman in the normal way
3◊ is a Transfer to 3♡
3♡ is a Transfer to 3♠

3♠ means I would have bid 3◇ had we not been playing Tranfers. (Some pairs play 3♠ as a minor suit slam suggestion. However, I feel it is more straightforward to use 3♠ as a diamond hand and then if you have clubs as well bid clubs on the next round. If you have clubs only you start with 3♣ and then bid 4♣ on the next round.)

The Response of 3◇ to 2NT

Responder guarantees at least five hearts and requests opener to rebid 3♡. Opener may break the Transfer if particularly suitable (e.g. 2NT–3◇–3♠) but this is very much the exception rather than the rule.

Responder holds:

1.	♠ 84	2NT	3◇
	♡ KJ1054	3♡	?
	◇ QJ5		
	♣ 754		

Bid 3NT. This gives opener the choice between 3NT and 4♡.

2.	♠ 84	2NT	3◇
	♡ KJ10543	3♡	?
	◇ QJ5		
	♣ 75		

Bid 4♡. With one more heart than already advertised and no ambitions above game level – raise to 4♡.

3.	♠ 84	2NT	3◇
	♡ KJ1054	3♠	?
	◇ AQ8		
	♣ 754		

Bid 4◇. Partner has broken the Transfer so he must be very suitable, perhaps ♠AKx ♡Axxxx ◇Kx ♣KQJ. Bid 4◇, cuebidding your ace.

4.	♠ 8	2NT	3◇
	♡ KJ1054	3♡	?
	◇ Q75		
	♣ AJ106		

Bid 4♣. Partner can still sign off in 4♡ but his hand might be something like ♠QJx ♡Ax ◇AKJx ♣KQ9x, when 6♣ would be a good spot.

The Response of 3♡ to 2NT
Responder now guarantees at least five spades and requires opener to rebid 3♠. The procedure is then similar to that described on page 82.

The Response of 3♠ to 2NT
As I have already indicated, this response is played in a number of different ways, but I suggest a simple and effective method is to treat it as a hand that would have replied 3◊ had you not been playing transfers. Let us look at the system in action on some difficult hands.

1.	♠ KJ5	♠ 84	West	East
	♡ AK64	♡ 53	2NT	3♠
	◊ KQ84	◊ AJ1075	4◊	5♣
	♣ AJ	♣ KQ82	6◊	Pass

After the first response there may be more than one route to 6◊, but it is essential for West to play the contract to protect his spade holding. The final contract is almost watertight. Declarer expects to make five diamonds, four clubs (discarding two spades), two hearts and one spade ruff.

2.	♠ KJ10	♠ 754	West	East
	♡ KQ8	♡ 5	2NT	3♠
	◊ K42	◊ AQJ1073	3NT	Pass
	♣ AKJ7	♣ Q64		

With only one ace and a minimum hand West signs off in 3NT. If West is only slightly better, say the ♠A instead of the ♠K (♠AJ10), then the ideal contract is unquestionably 6◊ by West. With the amended holding 6◊ by East would be in jeopardy on a spade lead while 6NT would leave West short of a trick on the same lead.

3.	♠ AJ10	♠ K743	West	East
	♡ QJ	♡ 43	2NT	3♠
	◊ K1074	◊ AQJ93	4◊	4♠
	♣ AKQ10	♣ J8	5♣	5◊
			Pass	

East's initial reaction is that 6◊, played by his partner, might be a good spot, so he sets the ball rolling with 3♠. West is quite happy with this development and duly bids 4◊, but it then becomes obvious that the heart holding is extremely delicate and 5◊ is the limit of the hand. At least they avoided the trap of playing in 3NT. A slight alteration to the West hand, with the points remaining the same, would make 6◊ by West virtually impregnable – give him ♡Kx instead of ♡QJ.

Here are some general notes and reminders

1. By playing Transfers over 1NT all you give up is the weakness takeout bid of 2◇. Not a great sacrifice for so much in return.

2. If the opponents double a 1NT bid all conventional aids such as Stayman, Transfers etc. are abandoned in order to allow responder to escape into any long suit.

3. With the use of Stayman and Transfers the immediate responses of 3♣, 3◇, 3♡ and 3♠ are going free. What should we do with them? Should they be weak (semi pre-emptive), invitational or strong? This is very much a matter for individual partnership preference. Twist my arm, and I would vote for strong – a good suit, slam suggestion.

4. Although I have dealt with Transfers only over a direct opening of 1NT or 2NT, it certainly makes sense to extend their use to analogous situations. For example (a) 2♣–2◇–2NT (b) 2♣–2◇–3NT, and perhaps after the overcall of 1NT. However, if experimenting with your toy for goodness sake ensure that your partner is on the same wavelength. You have been warned!

Clearly Transfers are not for the faint-hearted, but they open up so many avenues that it is hard to see serious-minded bridge players rejecting them for long. Perhaps the easiest way to get started is to play Transfers over 2NT only. Then, when you are familiar with the idea, gradually extend your repertoire.

Crowhurst

Star Rating: ✳✳

The Crowhurst convention, invented by Eric Crowhurst of Reading, Berkshire, the modern day Arch Priest of Acol, has found considerable favour amongst tournament players.

The idea is simple enough but extremely effective. Suppose you are playing a wide range no trump rebid, say 12-16 points, the bidding goes 1◇–1♠–1NT, and responder wishes to have more precise information, especially as to whether you are in the upper or lower point count bracket, then he asks the question with an artificial bid of 2♣ (Crowhurst): 1◇–1♠–1NT–2♣. Before enumerating the various responses that should be made by the opener, I would like to make it clear that wide range no trump rebids are not my cup of tea. I much prefer the traditional narrow range 15-16 point rebid. However, this is not the time to argue the merits of two playable methods, but one thing is for sure – if your system incorporates the wide range rebid then you must have an enquiry bid available for clarification. And what better than Crowhurst?

After opener has rebid 1NT, obviously responder will jump to game with a suitable hand and 13+ points, and raise to 2NT (invitational) on a straightforward hand of 11 points or perhaps a bare 12. But any hands of doubtful categorisation – and this would include those in the 10 or promising 9 point range – are better served by a Crowhurst enquiry. The bidding starts like this:

West	East
1◇	1♠
1NT(i)	2♣(ii)

(i) 12-16.
(ii) Crowhurst enquiry for range.

Basically, 2◇ shows a minimum range and 2NT a maximum, but there are some more informative replies that should take precedence over the standard responses when applicable. Remember that responder is prepared to settle in 2NT in the event of an unfavourable reply to his 2♣ enquiry, so this gives opener a small working area in which to be constructive.

While 15-16 points must be regarded as maximum and 12-13 minimum, opener will have to make his own mind up on 14, applying the general rules associated with intermediate cards (stuffing) and suit distribution. If in doubt maybe you should regard 14 as minimum.

With a minimum hand (12-13 points) these are opener's options:

$$1◇-1♠-1NT-2♣-?$$

1. Bid two of responder's suit to show three card support (2♠).
2. Bid two of a suit which has so far been concealed by the bidding (2♡).
3. Lacking either of the above, bid 2◇.

With a maximum hand (15-16 points) these are opener's options:

$$1◇-1♠-1NT-2♣-?$$

1. Jump to three in partner's suit to show three card support (3♠).
2. Jump to three in a suit which has so far been concealed by the bidding (3♡).
3. Jump to three in his own five card suit (3◇).
4. Lacking any of the above, bid 2NT.

Let us look at some examples:

(a)	♠ QJ4	♠ A10953	West	East
	♡ A6	♡ J74	1♢	1♠
	♢ AK85	♢ 62	1NT	2♣
	♣ J742	♣ KQ6	3♠	4♠
			Pass	

The right game contract is reached with the minimum fuss.

(b)	♠ 53	♠ A10742	West	East
	♡ KJ83	♡ Q1095	1♢	1♠
	♢ AQ1094	♢ KJ	1NT	2♣
	♣ AJ	♣ 63	3♡	4♡
			Pass	

Note how West is able to show the 'concealed' suit, and a maximum as well. This leaves East an easy task of just converting to game.

(c)	♠ 84	♠ AK752	West	East
	♡ K97	♡ QJ3	1♣	1♠
	♢ A109	♢ 5	1NT	2♣
	♣ AKJ95	♣ Q763	3♣	4♣
			4♢	4♠
			6♣	Pass

East's 2♣ bid is still Crowhurst despite the fact that West opened 1♣. 3♣ shows a maximum with five clubs, and 4♣ agrees the suit. 4♢ and 4♠ are cuebids leading to the excellent small slam.

(d)	♠ 105	♠ KQ72	West	East
	♡ KJ643	♡ Q105	1♡	1♠
	♢ AK3	♢ Q1094	1NT	2♣
	♣ Q64	♣ 109	2♡	Pass

No trouble in hitting the right spot.

(e)	♠ Q3	♠ J1086	West	East
	♡ A97	♡ K62	1♢	1♠
	♢ KQJ53	♢ A64	1NT	2♣
	♣ J83	♣ Q106	2♢	2NT
			Pass	

All avenues investigated and hopefully we will come to eight tricks.

(f) ♠ K108	♠ 63	West	East
♡ Q53	♡ AKJ74	1♣	1♡
◇ J42	◇ Q83	1NT	2♣
♣ AK75	♣ J42	2♡	Pass

Fairly safe, if unspectacular.

There is another situation, in my view by far the most valuable, where the Crowhurst convention is widely used. This is in the protective position. If you allow yourself the luxury of a wide range protective no trump, you will certainly cover a vast number of hands that might otherwise be difficult to bid. Let us say your agreed range is 11-15 points.

Partner enquires with 2♣ as before. In response, 2◇ indicates a minimum and 2NT maximum. Suit bids in between are minimum at the lowest level and maximum after a jump, but in both cases show a five carder.

♠ AQ5		♠ 72
♡ K10743	N	♡ QJ82
◇ 862	W E	◇ AK75
♣ KQ	S	♣ J83

West	North	East	South
–	1♠	Pass	Pass
1NT	Pass	2♣(i)	Pass
3♡	Pass	4♡	All Pass

(i) Crowhurst

With a maximum and a five card heart suit West gets the message across and an excellent game is reached. In fact ten tricks are not ironclad, especially if North finds a diamond lead, but only the supreme pessimist would wish to be less ambitious.

♠ K109		♠ A3
♡ Q76	N	♡ K102
◇ AQ85	W E	◇ J104
♣ 1096	S	♣ K8753

West	North	East	South
–	1♡	Pass	Pass
1NT	Pass	2♣(i)	Pass
2◇	Pass	2NT	All Pass

(i) Crowhurst

With a bit of luck we have stopped just in time. Perhaps this is the only hazard of Crowhurst. The very fact that the 1NT bid covers a wide range means that occasionally we will have to slam on the brakes and keep our fingers crossed that we won't skid off course. However, especially in the protective or balancing position, there is so much on the plus side that most players would willingly forgive the odd lurch in exchange for a meaningful conversation at other times.

Finally, a hand from actual match play. In a keenly contested head-to-head team match the cards fell like this:

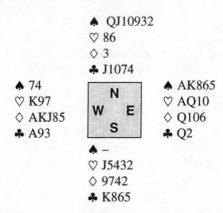

```
                          ♠ QJ10932
                          ♡ 86
                          ◇ 3
                          ♣ J1074
       ♠ 74                                  ♠ AK865
       ♡ K97          ┌─────────┐            ♡ AQ10
       ◇ AKJ85        │    N    │            ◇ Q106
       ♣ A93          │  W   E  │            ♣ Q2
                      │    S    │
                      └─────────┘
                          ♠ —
                          ♡ J5432
                          ◇ 9742
                          ♣ K865
```

In one room. East/West settled for 3NT. No risks, no hassle, plenty of tricks. At Game All, +660 seemd like a reasonable score.

In the other room there was a lot more action. This was the bidding:

West	North	East	South
1◇	Pass	1♠	Pass
1NT	Pass	2♣(i)	Pass
3◇	Pass	4◇	Pass
5♣	Pass	5♡	Pass
6◇	Pass	Pass	Dble
Pass	Pass	6NT	All Pass

(i) Crowhurst

After agreeing the suit and an exchange of cuebids, the East/West pair settled in the fine contract of 6◇. However, this was just the calm before the storm as South seized the opportunity to call for an unusual lead by making a Lightner double. Sensing that South must be void in spades, East rightly converted to 6NT.

North led the ♠Q which was won in dummy. With eleven tricks on top, the problem was how to develop one more. Of course, if North held the ♣K it would be easy but West reckoned that he would have overcalled 1♠ if he had the ♣K in addition to his good six-card spade suit. So the ♣K had to be credited to South which left just one viable plan – to find North with the ♣J10. However, nothing would be lost by playing a club to the ♣Q, for one trick had to be lost in any event.

So, after three rounds of diamonds declarer led the ♣3 towards dummy, but, as expected, South won the ♣K and returned a club. West won with the ace and cashed his red suit winners. This was the three-card ending:

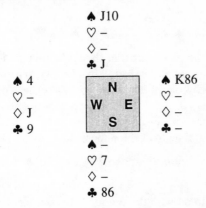

```
                ♠ J10
                ♡ –
                ◇ –
                ♣ J
   ♠ 4         ┌─────────┐      ♠ K86
   ♡ –         │    N    │      ♡ –
   ◇ J         │  W   E  │      ◇ –
   ♣ 9         │    S    │      ♣ –
              └─────────┘
                ♠ –
                ♡ 7
                ◇ –
                ♣ 86
```

When the ◇J was played North threw the ♣J. He really had no option for he certainly could not afford a spade and there was always the chance that his partner might hold the ♣9. In practice a happy West cashed the ♣9 and then the ♠K to land an exciting contract.

Just how much Crowhurst contributed to the success of this hand is difficult to estimate, but one fact is irrefutable – the pair using Crowhurst scored 1440 and that represented a swing of 13 IMPs.

Baron 2NT

Star Rating: ✳✳✳

When your partner opens the bidding and you have a strong hand, it is a moment to savour. Game will be on almost for certain. A small slam is possible. A grand slam – well, maybe. But one thing is for sure, good cards come your way only now and again, so when you strike lucky you want to have the machinery and the know how to get the maximum reward with the minimum risk.

Say partner opens 1♡ and you hold:

(a) ♠ 86
    ♡ KJ106
    ◇ AKJ97
    ♣ A10

(b) ♠ AKQ10865
    ♡ 6
    ◇ AK4
    ♣ 93

(c) ♠ AQ1074
    ♡ 63
    ◇ K
    ♣ AKJ65

(d) ♠ AK743
    ♡ 8
    ◇ AQ107
    ♣ KQ5

There is a certain basic procedure that should be followed when responding to your partner with a strong hand (16+ HCPs). With a fit in partner's suit, or a very powerful one suited hand, force at once – otherwise rebids will become extremely difficult. With a two suited misfit, don't force. Bid your suits naturally and await developments. With a three suited misfit, never force. You need time to develop the hand.

Thus, on hand (a) you should respond 3◇, on (b) 2♠ and on (c) and (d) 1♠.

So what has all this to do with the Baron 2NT, you ask? Not a lot, I must admit, but my plan was to set the scene so that I could then take you on to another hand:

(e)   ♠ AJ6
                    ♡ Q105
                    ◇ AQJ
                    ♣ QJ97

This hand does not fall into any of the categories we have discussed so far. In fact, if partner opens one of anything, it is not going to be easy to get your values as well as your hand type across to partner. You are too strong for an immediate or subsequent bid of 3NT, and too balanced to be involved in a number of suit bids. So there is a problem, but this problem quickly disappears if you are playing the Baron 2NT response which shows 16+ points balanced.

The Baron 2NT (a response to partner's opening in one of a suit)

The response of 2NT shows 16+ HCPs. The upper range is unlimited. The hand must be balanced, with no five card suit, so the shape will be 4-3-3-3 or 4-4-3-2. The following hands are all typical 2NT responses:

(1)	♠ AJ107	(2)	♠ K10	(3)	♠ Q107	(4)	♠ A6
	♡ KQ		♡ AQ5		♡ A84		♡ KQJ5
	◊ Q1096		◊ KQ82		◊ AJ96		◊ AJ10
	♣ AQ5		♣ KQ75		♣ KQ7		♣ AJ75

Playing this convention, all you have to give up is the natural response of 2NT which you would normally play as showing about 11 points – surely not too great a hardship. In any case, this restriction only applies if you have not yet passed. Passed hands automatically revert to their ordinary meaning as there is no way they could qualify for the 16+ HCP response.

Opener's Reaction to the Response of 2NT (1♣/1◊/1♡/1♠ – 2NT)

The basic idea is to bid as naturally as possible, but a reverse bid shows four cards in both suits:

1♡	2NT	3♠
1◊	2NT	3♡
1♣	2NT	3◊

So with five four in two suits opener must rebid the five card suit if it is lower ranking. This procedure facilitates the quest to locate a suitable fit. For example, let us say that the opener holds five diamonds and four hearts and the bidding starts 1◊–2NT. Now nothing is lost by rebidding 3◊. If responder has four hearts he will bid them over 3◊. Equally illuminating is when the bidding starts 1♡–2NT–3♠. Opener has four hearts and four spades. Clearly, when opener's suit lengths are 5-4, with the higher-ranking suit being the longer, he rebids naturally, i.e.

1♠	2NT	3♡
1♡	2NT	3◊
1◊	2NT	3♣

No trump rebids by opener should be informative and limited. Assuming the system caters for a weak no trump opening (12-14) with a stronger rebid (15-16) the rebid of 3NT over 2NT should also show 15-16 HCPs. Carrying this principle one step further, the rebid of 4NT (1◊–2NT–4NT) shows 17-18 HCPs and of course is forcing to at least a small slam (17 HCPs + 16 HCPs = 33 = small slam target).

Time to look at some hands.

	South	North
♠ AJ6	1♡	2NT
♡ Q105	3NT	4NT
◇ AQJ	6NT	Pass
♣ QJ97		

```
        ♠ AJ6
        ♡ Q105
        ◇ AQJ
        ♣ QJ97
♠ K72      N      ♠ 10953
♡ J986   W   E    ♡ 43
◇ 109863   S      ◇ 42
♣ 8               ♣ K6542
        ♠ Q84
        ♡ AK72
        ◇ K75
        ♣ A103
```

South's 3NT rebid showed 15-16 HCPs. North knew that the combined count was not less than 32, but he needed South to be maximum for the small slam to be a fair bet. 4NT expressed these feelings admirably. Looking at the four hands, we can see the good news and bad news just about level out. The black kings are well placed but neither clubs nor hearts break and there is duplication in diamonds. Anyway, West led the ◇10 which was won in dummy. The ♣Q won the second trick and was followed by a club to the ♣10, revealing the position. West threw a diamond. A spade to dummy's ♠J held, and the ♣A forced another diamond from West. Two top diamonds filled in a few more details and it only remained to try the hearts before executing the coup de grâce. This was the position, with South to lead, after the first ten tricks had fallen to declarer:

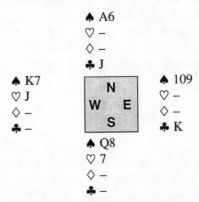

```
        ♠ A6
        ♡ –
        ◇ –
        ♣ J
♠ K7       N      ♠ 109
♡ J      W   E    ♡ –
◇ –        S      ◇ –
♣ –               ♣ K
        ♠ Q8
        ♡ 7
        ◇ –
        ♣ –
```

West's hand was like an open book. South graciously gave him his ♡J, but West could not avoid conceding two spade tricks in return.

The next hand was bid and played in competent style:

	♠ AK5	South	North
	♡ K843	1♡	2NT
	◇ AK8	3♡	4♡
	♣ J104	5♣	5◇

♠ 10986		♠ 743	5♡	6♡
♡ 10	**N**	♡ 752	Pass	
◇ J9653	**W E**	◇ Q107		
♣ KQ5	**S**	♣ 8732		

	♠ QJ2
	♡ AQJ96
	◇ 42
	♣ A96

The bidding was straightforward after North's response of 2NT (Baron). 3♡ showed five hearts, and 5♣ and 5◇ were cuebids. As South did not have spade control, he had to sign off in 5♡, but North not only had the spades bottled up, he also had something in reserve. Although 6♡ is completely cold as the cards lie, declarer needs to know exactly what he is doing before relinquishing the lead at the critical moment. The ♠10 was led. Declarer drew trumps, ruffed the third round of diamonds and cashed his spade winners, being careful to leave the lead in dummy. The ♣J was then run to West's ♣Q, leaving him in an unenviable position. If he returned a club, there would be no more club losers, while if he played anything else the ruff and discard would do just as well.

On my last hand it seemed that North/South had bitten off rather more than they could chew but fortunately their guardian angel was on duty.

	♠ 6	North	South
	♡ AK653	1♡	2NT(i)
	◇ KJ76	3◇ (ii)	4♣(iii)
	♣ K43	4♡(iii)	4♠(iii)

♠ KQ1085		♠ J743	5♣(iv)	5♡(v)
♡ 82	**N**	♡ J1097	5NT(vi)	7◇ (vii)
◇ 8532	**W E**	◇ 10		
♣ 107	**S**	♣ QJ85		

	♠ A92
	♡ Q4
	◇ AQ904
	♣ A962

    (i)   Baron showing 16+ points.

    (ii) North rebids 3♢ in the normal way because his suit lengths are in natural order.

    (iii) Cuebids. South's 4♣ must agree diamonds because he cannot have a five card suit and he certainly would not want to show a four card suit. To agree hearts he would have bid 3♡.

    (iv) Second round club control.

    (v) A vital filler.

    (vi) Grand Slam Force. Bid seven with two of top three trumps.

    (vii)Trusting and obedient.

Getting to the grand slam was one thing, making it was something else. On top there are four diamonds, one spade, two spade ruffs, three hearts and two clubs, a total of twelve tricks. The red suits broke poorly; diamonds 3-2 would have made it easy for declarer to set up the fifth heart. Let's see what happened:

West led the ♠K. Declarer won and ruffed a spade. The ♢K drew East's ten and a diamond to the the nine confirmed the break. A second spade ruff was followed by a heart to the queen and the ♢A, leaving:

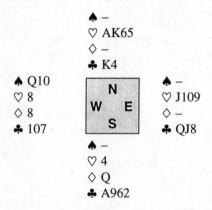

When the last trump was drawn, dummy threw the ♡5 but East was in dire trouble. He was squeezed. In practice, he threw the ♣8, but it really did not matter. Whatever he did was going to be wrong and declarer was not going to be denied his moment of glory.

There is no doubt that the Baron 2NT is a useful and exciting convention to play. It fills an awkward gap in a natural system and is therefore to be thoroughly recommended.

6
DOUBLES

Negative or Sputnik Doubles

Star Rating: Played on a mini scale: ✳✳✳✳✳
                Played extensively: ✳✳✳

'How did Sputnik get into the act?' you might well ask. Sputnik, a Soviet earth satellite, means (well, roughly, anyway) 'travelling companion' and that seems to have nothing to do with doubles in any shape or form. But wait a moment. In the late fifties Alvin Roth of New York, one of the great theorists of our time, conceived the idea that when the opposition intervened at a low level there was more to be gained by using a double for takeout, or in a negative sense, than for punitive purposes as in standard methods. And what better name for this brainchild than Sputnik, because at that time there was much talk about the first Soviet Sputnik circling the skies. So we have Sputnik Doubles and Negative Doubles meaning one and the same thing, although perhaps Negative Doubles is the term most commonly used today. Such Doubles are usually made on fairly balanced hands and are especially useful when playing five card majors, although this is by no means a prerequisite.

Let's see the idea in action. Your partner, West, opens 1♣ and North intervenes with 1♠. You are East and hold:

♠ 1054
♡ K1086
♢ A974
♣ 83

In standard methods, where a Double would now be for penalties, you are scuppered and would have to pass. Playing Negative Doubles you are on firm ground. You double, showing the values to respond at the one level (6 or 7+ points), a guarantee of four cards in the unbid major and some support for any unbid suit – in this case diamonds.

After a Negative Double the opener should support the major suit shown by the Double whenever he has them. He raises quantitively, always allowing for his partner's bid to have been made on minimum values, e.g.

West	West	North	East	South
♠ Q3	1♣	1♠	Double	Pass
♡ Q753	2♡			
◇ Q8				
♣ AK1098				

Replace the ◇ 8 with the ◇ K and the rebid should be 3♡. Make the hand stronger still, replacing the ♡3 with the ♡A while still retaining the king of diamonds, and the rebid should be 4♡.

All West's rebids are non-forcing (remember, he can rebid no trumps quantitatively, rebid his own suit or another suit at minimum level), so if he wants the auction to continue he must cuebid the suit in which the opponents have overcalled. Of course, East may not be minimum at all. He may have quite a good hand (11+ points) in which case he will express the fact by continuing the dialogue.

Sputnik Doubles work just as effectively when an opponent intervenes at the two level. However, the doubler will now have to be a little stronger. Nine plus points is about right.

Your partner, West, opens 1 ◇ and North bids 2♠. East holds:

♠ 75
♡ AQ83
◇ 752
♣ K1074

A negative double says it all.

Equally, when major suits have been bid a Negative Double should show support for the minors. West opens 1♡ and North comes in with 1♠. Now when East doubles he is showing support for both diamonds and clubs. The double can be made on about seven plus points, but if the sequence has started 1♠–2♡–Double, then the doubler should hold nine plus points.

There seems little point in using a Negative Double to show spades in the sequence 1♣/1◇–1♡–? when you can quite easily bid the suit yourself (some players double to show four spades and bid the suit to show five).

A better idea is for the Negative Double to *deny* four spades and show four or five cards in the other minor, perhaps with insufficient values to introduce the suit at the two level.

	West	North
	1♦	1♥

East holds:

(a) ♠ 74	(b) ♠ 863	(c) ♠ 1063	(d) ♠ 106
♡ 8753	♡ 7532	♡ 85	♡ 974
◇ K6	◇ K9	◇ Q85	◇ Q106
♣ A10742	♣ KJ107	♣ AQ542	♣ AJ1075

Double in each case.

With the following hands you should bid naturally:

(a) ♠ K1063	(b) ♠ J106	(c) ♠ 86	(d) ♠ QJ6
♡ 8742	♡ AJ9	♡ 10743	♡ 753
◇ Q106	◇ 1063	◇ K1075	◇ K6
♣ Q3	♣ K532	♣ A72	♣ AQJ107
Bid 1♠	Bid 1NT	Bid 2◇	Bid 2♣

Perhaps you are beginning to think that the Negative Double is the panacea for all opposition intervention and, indeed, that is the way many tournament players see it, extending its use to the three and even four level. Well, far be from me to dampen the enthusiasm of those who want to go all the way with their toy, but it is very essential to agree the level at which your Negative Double ends and your Penalty Double begins.

If you are a rubber bridge player you may be saying, 'But what about my penalty Doubles – often so profitable at low levels?' Many a large gin and tonic is earned by clobbering the opponents for their indiscretions at the two level. My old friend Zia Mahmood tells me that Negative Doubles are all the rage in America today, even in rubber bridge circles, and are gaining ground worldwide. In rubber bridge clubs in the UK, or at least in the clubs in which I play, Negative Doubles have not yet emerged. If the opposition intervene and you double, that is for blood. Change will not come easily although it is no doubt only a question of time. Rubber bridge players who are worried that their juicy penalties may one day be taken from them, as Negative Doubles gain popularity, can take solace from the tournament players who would no doubt claim that they actually have their cake and eat it too.

What happens is this. Whenever possible the opener is expected to re-open with a double after his partner has passed, often on values that would give traditionalists an acute feeling of unilateralism. As West you hold:

♠ AKJ53
♡ 6
♢ KJ97
♣ 974

You open 1♠, North bids 2♡, East and South pass ... and you? You double, of course! The idea is that with values South would have bid whereas East may have been unable to do so. East is supposed to hold something like:

♠ 42
♡ KJ984
♢ A32
♣ Q105

and naturally passes your re-opening Double with confidence. When it works like this, Negative Doublers certainly have the best of all worlds.

If you are new to Negative Doubles and want to start practising them, without putting the whole machinery into operation at once, you might like to begin like this:

Partner bids	Next player bids	You bid
1♣ or 1♢	1♡	?

Double denies four spades and shows the other minor (four or five cards) with 6 to a poor 9 points.

1♣ or 1♢	1♠	?

Double shows four hearts, tolerance for the other minor and 6+ points. Also five hearts with 6 to a poor 9 points.

1♡	1♠	?

Double shows 6+ points with both minors.

One of a suit (say 1♡)	Two of a suit (say 2♢)	?

Double is for penalty.

This mini approach, where doubles at the two level and above are penalties, will allow you to familiarise yourself with the machinery and take more on board when you are ready to do so.

Competitive Doubles

Star Rating: ✳✳✳✳

A Competitive Double, as the name implies, is a Double used in a competitive situation, primarily for takeout, that asks partner to re-assess in light of information expressed by the Double.

As with most forms of negative Double the maximum benefit is derived during low level exchanges and especially, but not exclusively, when the opponents have supported each other in the same suit. Here are some of the most useful ways in which the Competitive Double can be used.

Partner (East) overcalls – opponents agree a suit.

(a)	West	West	North	East	South
	♠ 7		1♣	1♠	2♣
	♡ AJ853	?			
	◊ KJ642				
	♣ 84				

(b)	West	West	North	East	South
	♠ AQ742		1♡	2◊	2♡
	♡ 8	?			
	◊ 104				
	♣ Q10985				

(c)	West	West	North	East	South
	♠ A10976		1◊	2♣	2◊
	♡ KQ1084	?			
	◊ 10				
	♣ 104				

In each case West should double, showing length in the unbid suits. There would be little mileage in playing such Doubles for penalty so it is only sensible to employ them in a more useful role – defined as Competitive Doubles. Of course, all partnerships should agree on the level to which their Competitive Double applies. Up to 3♡ may be a reasonable compromise but a number of tournament players take them even further.

There are so many situations in which a Competitive Double can be invaluable that it is hardly surprising that so many tournament players have adopted this gadget and use it extensively. Perhaps, like all good conventions, it is over used. What you need to ask yourself is this: 'If I am going to adopt a Competitive Double in situation X, am I going to lose out by discarding a penalty Double?' Where the opponents have bid and supported one another, one seldom loses by preferring a Competitive Double.

Playing pairs you hold as West:

♠	A83
♡	K95
◇	QJ75
♣	632

The bidding proceeds like this:

West	North	East	South
–	–	1♡	1♠
2♡	2♠	Pass	Pass
?			

Maybe 2♡ would not have been your choice on the first round but it is probably as good, or as bad, as anything else. Anyway, what are you going to do now? Playing Competitive Doubles you have an easy decision. Double and leave it to partner. You are showing him a maximum with only three hearts – with four you could continue to 3♡ yourself. Hopefully he will be able to arrive at the right answer. In a slightly different setting you might make the same Competitive Double and find partner only too delighted to pass for penalties once you show something extra.

Now let's look at another situation:

(a)

West		West	North	East	South
♠	Q8		1♡	1♠	2◇
♡	A4	?			
◇	873				
♣	K109863				

(b)

West		West	North	East	South
♠	J63		1♣	1◇	1♠
♡	K10986	?			
◇	K4				
♣	Q104				

(c)

West		West	North	East	South
♠	AJ1074	–	1◇	1♡	2♣
♡	J10	?			
◇	754				
♣	K107				

In each case West should double. When three suits have been bid, Double by the fourth player (Competitive) shows interest in the unbid suit and tolerance for partner's suit. Although the urge to play Competitive Doubles in the above three situations may not be as strong as when the opponents support one another, nevertheless it is almost certainly the most beneficial arrangement. It is also worth remembering that the penalty element may not have disappeared entirely. With a suitable hand partner may opt to pass, or wield the axe should his RHO rebid his first suit.

Using Competitive Doubles, responder is well placed in this sort of situation:

West	North	East	South
1♣	Pass	1♠	2◇
Pass	Pass	?	

East holds:

♠ K10643	or	♠ K10643
♡ AJ5		♡ A854
◇ 84		◇ 8
♣ Q72		♣ 732

A bid of 2♡ by East should be reserved for a 'playing' hand, maybe 5-5 in the majors. However, by doubling he gets the message across that he has enough high cards to want to compete. Opener now a decision; he can introduce a new suit, rebid his own suit, support partner's suit or pass hoping to collect a penalty.

There is yet another way in which a Competitive Double can come to your rescue. This is when you use it as a game try (strange to think that Jeremy Flint and I wrote about this in *Tiger Bridge* some thirty years ago). I admit that this form of Competitive Double does not rate highly in the frequency stakes but when it does occur it can be worth a million dollars. Give it the five star treatment for there is no way that it can cost.

Suppose you are West and hold:

| ♠ AQ7 |
| ♡ AJ1084 |
| ◇ 8 |
| ♣ A653 |

You open 1♡ and then the bidding proceeds like this:

West	North	East	South
1♡	2◇	2♡	3◇
?			

Do you see what has happened? There is no room for you to make a game try. If the opposition had not been so busy (1♡–Pass–2♡–Pass) you would probably have bid 3♣ over 2♡, urging partner to 4♡ with a suitable hand and help in clubs. That would have been neat and tidy. Of course, you could now bid 3♡ but that is exactly the bid you would make when you wanted to buy the contract at the lowest level possible. And

how is partner to distinguish between 'I want to play in 3♡ so for goodness sake don't bid on' and: 'This is a game try – I want you to bid 4♡ if
you are maximum and suitable'? The answer is – he does not have to.
Using Competitive Doubles, you now double over 3◊. That is your game
try. Thus when you advance to 3♡ in the sequence given the message is
unequivocal. You wish to play there and partner is expected to pass.

Suppose you opt for the Competitive Double, as indeed you would on the
above hand, partner will normally convert to 3♡ or 4♡, depending on
suitability. However, a new option has been created. Perhaps East holds a
hand like this:

♠ K5
♡ 9763
◊ KJ107
♣ 842

in which case he will happily pass your (takeout) double and play for
penalties. Let's look at a hand:

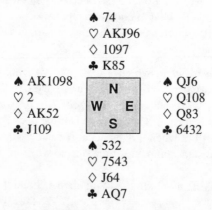

♠ 74
♡ AKJ96
◊ 1097
♣ K85

♠ AK1098   ♠ QJ6
♡ 2   ♡ Q108
◊ AK52   ◊ Q83
♣ J109   ♣ 6432

♠ 532
♡ 7543
◊ J64
♣ AQ7

There was some spirited bidding on this hand from a large pairs competition with plus scores going both ways. 3♠ just made was good for
East/West while 4♠ resulted in a plus for North/South. One East/West
pair playing Competitive Doubles judged most successfully when at Love
All the bidding went like this:

West	North	East	South
1♠	2♡	2♠	3♡
Double	All Pass		

East reasoned that they were unlikely to make 4♠ but that his ♡Q108 might produce an unexpected trick so a pass had much to commend it. How right he was! Collecting two spades, three diamonds and one heart for a score of +300 was not difficult. Maybe they were a little lucky because with a slight alteration in the minor suits North would have gone only one down, but then West might well have had trouble in making more than eight tricks in spades. Anyway, in the event the defenders were very happy with both their gadget and the result!

Naturally, if you play Competitive Doubles then you have to give up the immediate penalty Double in all those situations where Competitive Doubles apply. But as we have seen so far, we have been able to use the Competitive Double as a game try – leaving partner with the option of transferring into a penalty Double if that suits him best. We have been able to contest the bidding at a low level in comparative safety (after partner has overcalled) because we have been able to show both our suits without bidding higher or taking a unilateral view. And where three suits have been bid we've been able to show interest in the fourth suit and tolerance for partner's suit. When responding with two suits, yet not strong enough to bid the second one after interference, we've still found a way of getting our message across. Finally, we were in a position to show a maximum raise to the two level with only three trumps and an urge to do something more. All that can't really be bad!

Responsive Doubles

Star Rating: ✳✳✳

Superficially, Responsive Doubles give the immediate impression of passing the buck, or suffering an acute attack of indecision. North opens the bidding with one of a suit, East doubles for takeout, South raises his partner's suit and now West doubles for takeout. West's bid is a Responsive Double.

This has been the bidding so far:

West	North	East	South
–	1♡	Double	2♡
Double			

There are two sound reasons for using a Responsive Double:

1. Hands suitable for penalising the opponents at a low level when they have agreed a suit are rare.

2. The responder to a takeout Double does not always have a clearcut choice. Suppose West holds the following hand and the bidding has proceeded as above but it is still West to call:

♠ 74
♡ 1083
◇ K1075
♣ A1064

Should West bid 3♣ or 3◇? In an ideal world it probably wouldn't matter much because East would have four cards in each minor, something like:

♠ AJ83
♡ 6
◇ A963
♣ K875

However, we all know that in real life partner will sometimes have less than an ideal holding in one of the minors while being well stocked in the other, say:

♠ AJ83
♡ 62
◇ AQ96
♣ K75

It may now be crucial to locate the best fit and that is exactly what a Responsive Double sets out to do.

Responsive Doubles are usually played at the two and three level when there is no clearcut decision to make. Strength should be appropriate for play at the level to which the responsive doubler invites his partner to bid (minimum, usually 6-9 points).

More often than not the responsive doubler will be denying a five card suit, and his suit lengths – those that he is offering – will be roughly the same. If it were otherwise he would hardly have a problem needing further clarification. Where a major suit has been bid a Responsive Double (1♡–Double–2♡–Double) should deny four cards in the other major. Where a minor suit has been bid a Responsive Double normally shows four cards in both majors.

Let's look at some hands.

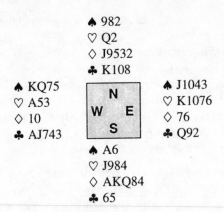

♠ 982
♡ Q2
◇ J9532
♣ K108

♠ KQ75
♡ A53
◇ 10
♣ AJ743

N
W E
S

♠ J1043
♡ K1076
◇ 76
♣ Q92

♠ A6
♡ J984
◇ AKQ84
♣ 65

Playing rubber bridge, after an initial pass by East, South opened 1◇, West doubled for takeout and North raised to 2◇. This was the moment of truth for East. Playing normal rubber bridge restricted conventions, his choice was limited to two of a major or pass. Not unreasonably, he chose 2♡. South bid one more diamond and West one more heart and that was where the matter rested. Final contract, 3♡ by East. Although East put up a spirited struggle he could not avoid the loss of five tricks (one spade, two hearts and one in each minor). Of course, it was obvious that a spade contract would have fared very much better, nine tricks being easy and ten a possibility. Had Responsive Doubles been permitted, then East could have doubled over Two Diamonds and the spade fit would have emerged.

This was a hand from a pairs tournament:

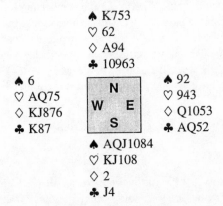

♠ K753
♡ 62
◇ A94
♣ 10963

♠ 6
♡ AQ75
◇ KJ876
♣ K87

N
W E
S

♠ 92
♡ 943
◇ Q1053
♣ AQ52

♠ AQJ1084
♡ KJ108
◇ 2
♣ J4

As so often happens in pairs events, especially those of a not very high standard, the results were extremely varied. North/South achieved a good score when they were allowed to play in 3♠ – just making. East/West did well when given the chance to double 4♠, but 4◇ just made was also well rewarded. The East/Wests who did really badly were those who played in 4♣. After 1♠–Double, North bid either 2♠ or 3♠, depending on style, and East was in the hot seat. Those Easts who were playing Responsive Doubles were completely at ease. They doubled and the right spot was soon found (South 3♠–West 4◇–All Pass). But spare a thought for those unfortunate Easts who had to guess whether to pass, or bid 3♣ or 4♣ depending on the level of North's raise.

Against a contract of 4♣ the defence was unrelenting. South led his singleton diamond to his partner's ace. The *nine* of diamonds was returned (McKenney asking for a spade back) and ruffed, and then a second diamond ruff was obtained when South underled his ace of spades for partner to win the king. The defence still hand to score one heart and one natural trump trick for three down – instead of making ten tricks in diamonds!

Just in case you think it is all one way traffic, there will be occasions when you will undoubtedly wish that you were *not* playing Responsive Doubles.

This is what you hold as West:

♠ 863
♡ QJ108
◇ A95
♣ 1052

The bidding starts:

West	North	East	South
–	1♡	Double	3♡
?			

Of course, you would dearly like to double for penalties ... but you can't. It's tough but you must pass. As with any conventional bid it is difficult to have the best of all worlds all the time. What matters is that you obtain sensible results most of the time; besides, on a good day your partner might double again, and then you'll certainly know what to do. Hopefully you've passed at normal tempo so that there is no question of an ethical problem....

Lightner Doubles

Star Rating: ✳✳✳✳✳

The opponents have just bid an uncontested small slam in a suit and with your two aces, or one ace and some other goodies, you think you may beat it. Do you double? If you do you are laying heavy odds on your judgement being right. After all, you are unlikely to gain more than an extra 50 points (or 100 vulnerable) but your loss can be several times that amount – quite apart from the risk of a redouble. S. J. Simon covered this aspect of doubling fully and convincingly in his great classic *Why You Lose at Bridge*. Serious-minded bridge players are left in no doubt that it is both wrong and unprofitable to double a freely bid slam in a suit because you hold two aces, or because you hold a few values that might result in the contract going one down.

This brings us to the Lightner Double, invented by Theodore Lightner of New York as long ago as 1929. His idea was this. If competent opponents bid freely to a slam – not as a sacrifice but with obvious expectations of making it – it is fair to assume that they will fulfil their contract or go one down so there is little to be gained by a penalty Double. Therefore a Double by the hand not on lead should have a conventional meaning – 'Partner, please find an unusual lead'. The most frequent reason for this is that the doubler is void of a suit and wishes to score an immediate ruff.

The Lightner Double automatically bars the lead of any suit bid by the defence in a normal competitive sequence or, of course, a trump. If the opposition have bid three suits a defender should not double if he wants the lead of the unbid suit. Many players insist on the lead of dummy's first bid side suit or, if dummy has failed to bid a side suit, the first bid side suit by declarer. However, in the final analysis the player on lead must find something unusual and naturally he will look favourably on a long suit of his own that perhaps partner will be able to ruff. If in doubt play dummy's first bid side suit.

Let's look at a hand:

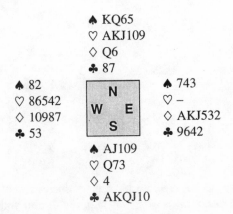

```
              ♠ KQ65
              ♡ AKJ109
              ◇ Q6
              ♣ 87
  ♠ 82                        ♠ 743
  ♡ 86542        N            ♡ -
  ◇ 10987     W     E         ◇ AKJ532
  ♣ 53           S            ♣ 9642
              ♠ AJ109
              ♡ Q73
              ◇ 4
              ♣ AKQJ10
```

West	North	East	South
–	–	–	1♣
Pass	1♡	2◊	2♠
Pass	5♠	Pass	6♠
Pass	Pass	Double	All Pass

Whether East bids 2◊ or not makes little difference. His final Double says it all. Lead something unusual, not my suit (if he has bid) and not the unbid suit (if he hasn't). Playing the Lightner Double, West won't have to be a genius to find a heart lead (dummy's first bid suit, by the way). It is worth noting that the East/West gain was not just an extra 50 for one down doubled, although that is what will appear on the scoresheet, but in reality 1080 (500 for slam, 300 for game, 180 for 6♠ plus 100 penalty) because without East's Double West would no doubt have led the ◊10 and the slam would have succeeded.

On the next hand East took steps to ensure that he got the right lead by paving the way early on. At least this avoided any ambiguity.

Game All. Dealer South.

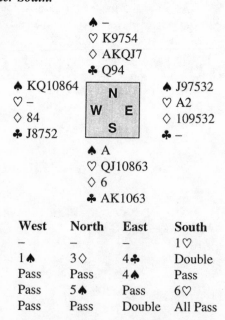

```
              ♠ –
              ♡ K9754
              ◊ AKQJ7
              ♣ Q94
♠ KQ10864                    ♠ J97532
♡ –           ┌─────────┐    ♡ A2
◊ 84          │ N       │    ◊ 109532
♣ J8752       │ W   E   │    ♣ –
              │    S    │
              └─────────┘
              ♠ A
              ♡ QJ10863
              ◊ 6
              ♣ AK1063
```

West	North	East	South
–	–	–	1♡
1♠	3◊	4♣	Double
Pass	Pass	4♠	Pass
Pass	5♠	Pass	6♡
Pass	Pass	Double	All Pass

On a spade lead declarer would have made his contract in comfort but West was in no doubt as to what was required of him and dutifully led a club. Once East had scored his ruff the defence had no further interest except for the ace of trumps but they had every reason to feel pleased with their result. In fact 6♠ would have been remarkably cheap but who wants a cheap save when the alternative is a plus score?

Of course, on this occasion East did not bid clubs 'in a *normal* competitive sequence', so there was no question of excluding that suit. On the contrary, he went out of his way to make it crystal clear that West should lead a club. Let us suppose for a moment that East, instead of bidding 4♣, bid 4♠ and that North/South continued directly to 6♡. Now when East doubles West may ponder over his lead. Something unusual, not a spade. So what? Dummy's first suit was diamonds, but can East really want a diamond lead? With only two in his own hand that seems most improbable, so no doubt West will arrive at the right conclusion. However, East's antics, designed to make life easy for partner, are worth noting.

Perhaps I should conclude with a hand that contains an ominous warning for the unwary:

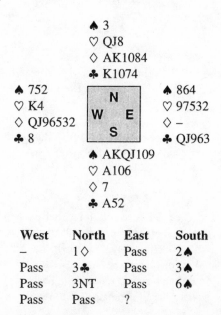

	♠ 3	
	♡ QJ8	
	◇ AK1084	
	♣ K1074	

♠ 752		♠ 864
♡ K4		♡ 97532
◇ QJ96532		◇ –
♣ 8		♣ QJ963

	♠ AKQJ109	
	♡ A106	
	◇ 7	
	♣ A52	

West	North	East	South
–	1◇	Pass	2♠
Pass	3♣	Pass	3♠
Pass	3NT	Pass	6♠
Pass	Pass	?	

You are East. Are you tempted to double? Of course you would like a diamond lead and it seems quite likely that partner has got a trick somewhere, but what about your defence to 6NT? Not good, and that's an understatement. Don't forget the opposition also know what you are up to when you double. On this occasion no trumps have already been suggested once and South will surely remove to 6NT if you warn him of the impending danger. So, grit your teeth, pass and hope partner will find the right lead. They do sometimes.

Striped-Tail Ape Double

Star Rating: ✳

I have to admit that the Striped-tail Ape Double is not an everyday occurrence, and thus you may have to wait a while before you have the opportunity to practise this exciting coup. So, if you'll excuse the mixed metaphor a rare bird it may be, but what a plumage when you see it in full flight! Let me set the scene. At game to North/South, North opens the bidding with 1♢. East, your partner, bids 1♠ and South shows his muscles with 2♠. You, West, hold this unappetising collection:

♠ Q109542
♡ 753
♢ 6
♣ 842

What to do for the best? Rightly or wrongly, you bid 4♠. This brings 4NT from North, a pass from East and 5♢ from South.

It's back to you:

West	North	East	South
–	1♢	1♠	2♠
4♠	4NT	Pass	5♢
?			

Suppose you double. Yes, I know it is for penalties and you have not a hope in hell of defeating them, but as a result of your apparent eccentric optimism one of two things is likely to happen: (a) North passes, hardly able to believe his good fortune or (b) North, who is not the sort of person to be intimidated or short changed, redoubles. That is your cue to retreat to 5♠, or in other words, flee like a Striped-Tail Ape!

This is the full hand:

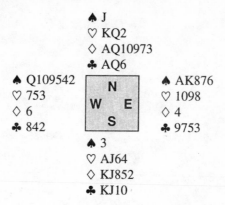

```
                    ♠ J
                    ♡ KQ2
                    ◇ AQ10973
                    ♣ AQ6
  ♠ Q109542        ┌─────────┐        ♠ AK876
  ♡ 753            │    N    │        ♡ 1098
  ◇ 6              │ W     E │        ◇ 4
  ♣ 842            │    S    │        ♣ 9753
                   └─────────┘
                    ♠ 3
                    ♡ AJ64
                    ◇ KJ852
                    ♣ KJ10
```

The mathematics (duplicate scoring) are interesting:

    5◇, doubled and made + 1 = 950
    6◇ bid and made   = 1370
    5♠, doubled – 5   = 1100

We can see from this example that the best result obtainable on this particular hand is the first one – a swing of 9 IMPs when the other pair in
your team bid to 6◇.

So the Striped-Tail Ape Double (usually of game) is an inhibitory shock
tactic manoeuvre made when a player feels sure his opponents are going
to bid and make a slam; the doubled contract with overtricks scoring less
than bidding a successful slam. If the opposition redouble then the doubler flees like a Striped-Tail Ape to his own comparatively safe haven.

Does this gambit work? In theory, in a tough and enlightened world of
seasoned players, there is no very good reason for such tactics to cause
more than a ripple. But bridge has a strong emotional and psychological
side to it. These very elements sometimes play funny tricks which beggar
all logical explanation – even at exalted levels, as we shall see.

In the 1969 British Trials for the European Championships the following
hand gave the spectators and journalists a considerable amount of plea-
sure. Although personally involved my memory of the exact details was a
little hazy, so I must acknowledge with thanks the amusing account relat-
ed by Terence Reese in his entertaining book *Bridge at the Top*.

North/South Game. IMPs. Dealer South.

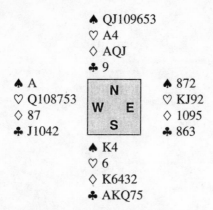

```
                    ♠ QJ109653
                    ♡ A4
                    ◇ AQJ
                    ♣ 9
      ♠ A              N            ♠ 872
      ♡ Q108753                    ♡ KJ92
      ◇ 87         W     E         ◇ 1095
      ♣ J1042                      ♣ 863
                     S
                    ♠ K4
                    ♡ 6
                    ◇ K6432
                    ♣ AKQ75
```

South opened 1◇, West (Freddie North) bid 3♡ and North, who appears to have a number of options, may well have hit the nail on the head when he bid 5♠. East (John Pugh) was reasonably certain that the opposition could make a slam so he doubled 5♠! Everyone passed, perhaps in various degrees of happiness and doubt, and North duly collected his twelve tricks for a score of 1050. So far so good, Pugh had produced the striped-tail ape at just the right moment and it only remained for our other pair, Nico Gardener and Tony Priday, to bid the slam for a nice swing (+1430).

Unfortunately the Gardener/Priday wires got crossed because they reached 7♠, doubled. So the expected swing occurred – but not in the direction generally anticipated! Boris Schapiro, who had been kibitzing, lived up to his name of the Joker (given to him by Guy Ramsey in 'Aces All') when he later announced to a crowded room 'Priday and Gardener were unlucky on one hand. They bid a grand slam and the ace of trumps was on the wrong side. Bad luck. Could happen to anyone!'

Despite this unfortunate setback (the operation was a success but the patient died) the Striped-Tail Ape Double has a definite place in your tool kit – but don't expect to reach for it too often.

7

COMPETITIVE BIDDING

In the modern game, competition is fierce. The opposition are always making nuisances of themselves. Intervening where previously they would have left well alone. If they are going to put themselves around, we will need counter measures. The take-out double is a big help, but there are other aides that can be adopted. We will look at some of these in this chapter. If the opposition are going to be so inconsiderate that they meddle in our auctions, then the least we can do is return the compliment. We will look at some tools that may prove useful in that respect too.

The Lebensohl Convention

Star Rating: ✷✷

The Lebensohl Convention is designed to allow you greater accuracy and expression after your right-hand opponent (RHO) intervenes over your partner's 1NT opening bid (1NT–2♡–?). Before we look at the benefits that derive from Lebensohl, let us first look at standard methods.

Partner, North, opens 1NT and East overcalls in a suit. Options available to South under standard methods:

(a) 2NT does not promise a stopper in East's suit, just the number of points necessary for the bid.

(b) 3NT does not promise a stopper in East's suit, just the number of points necessary for the bid.

(c) A suit bid at the lowest level shows length, but is non-forcing (e.g. 1NT–2♡–3◇).

(d) A jump bid is forcing to game (e.g. 1NT–2◇–3♠).

(e) A cuebid in East's suit takes the place of Stayman. 1NT–2♡–3♡ would show four spades and values for game, while 1NT–2◇–3◇ would guarantee at least one four card major and values for game.

(f) Double is for penalties.

That is certainly a playable method and, indeed, has to suffice in many a bridge club in this country today. One must admit though it is a little rough at the edges. Sophistication is limited and from time to time guess-work will be at a premium.

The Lebensohl Convention, invented by George Boehm of New York, was designed to give greater definition to responder's hand after partner opens 1NT and RHO intervenes. The mechanism varies somewhat depending on whether the overcall is made at the two level or three level and also whether it shows one suit or two. The cornerstone of this convention is that respon-der's bid of 2NT (1NT–2♡–2NT) is artificial and requires the opener to reply 3♣. Responder can now pass 3♣, if that is where he wants to play, or bid his suit, which is non-forcing. It follows that suit bids at the three level, without using the Lebensohl 2NT, are forcing. (1NT–2♠–3♢ is forcing.)

As with all gadgets, if a specific bid is harnessed to a conventional mean-ing, you can no longer use that bid in its natural sense. So if you play Lebensohl you have to forgo the natural limit raise of 2NT. If that, quite understandably, perturbs you, all is not lost. You can use a Double (1NT–2♡–Double) as your 2NT limit raise. Superficially, that might seem like a poor exchange since you can no longer penalise RHO for an indis-cretion, but closer examination refutes this argument. There are bound to be hands where, pre-Lebensohl, you would have made a quantitative raise to 2NT only to find that partner, now aware of your limited wealth, would have liked to take a penalty. Now with Lebensohl in your armoury your Double, although not penalty orientated, gives partner that option.

Before I summarise the responses over both one-suited and two-suited overcalls there are two more important bids to remember.

2NT (Lebensohl) followed by 3NT over partner's 3♣ shows a stop in the enemy suit:

| 1NT | 2♠ | 2NT | Pass |
| 3♣ | Pass | 3NT | Pass |

while a direct jump to 3NT:

| 1NT | 2♠ | 3NT | Pass |

denies a stopper in their suit.

Partner, North, opens 1NT and East overcalls with a natural bid of 2♡. South's actions summarised:

	1NT	2♡	?

2♠	Natural, competitive and non-forcing.
3♣	Natural and forcing.
3◇	Natural and forcing.
3♠	Natural and forcing.
3♡	Stayman (showing four spades, no stopper in opposition suit, forcing to game).
2NT	Followed by 3♡ over 3♣, Stayman (four spades) with a stopper in their suit.
2NT	Followed by 3NT promises stopper in their suit.

1NT	2♡	2NT	Pass
3♣	Pass	3NT	

3NT	No stopper in enemy suit.

1NT	2♡	3NT	Pass

Double A natural raise to 2NT (occasionally South may double on a stronger hand, in which case South can control the subsequent auction). Partner can always 'convert' to a penalty double by passing if that seems desirable.

Cuebids and jump bids short of game are, of course, forcing.

Partner, North, opens 1NT and East overcalls at the three level. South's actions summarised.

1NT	3 any	?

A suit bid at the three level is forcing to game.

Double: This bid is negative and promises support for any suit not shown by the overcall. It is not necessarily forcing to game.

Partner, North, opens 1NT and East overcalls conventionally, showing two suits (say 2♣, Landy, showing the majors). South's actions summarised:

1NT	2♣ (majors)	?

Double Penalty orientated in at least one of the suits shown by the overcall.

2◇	A two-level bid in a suit not shown by the overcall is non-forcing.
3♣	Forcing to game.

3◇   Forcing to game.

2♡   A cuebid in the lower of the two suits shown by the overcall (spades and hearts) is not forcing to game.

2♠   A cuebid in the higher of the two suits shown by the overcall is game forcing.

2NT   Requests partner to bid 3♣. South can now pass 3♣ or bid three of his suit which is non-forcing. If South bids 3NT over 3♣ he shows stops in both suits shown by the overcall.

3NT   South may have a stop in one of the suits shown by the overcall, but denies stops in both.

A conventional overcall identifying one suit only (Astro, for example, where 2◇ shows spades and another suit) is handled as follows:

Double Suggests the values to double 2♠.

2♠   Shows values in the other three suits.

2NT and other bids are used in the same sense as in the above examples.

Let us look at a few hands:

North opens 1NT (12-14 points), East overcalls 2◇), natural. South holds:

(a) ♠ AJ1074
     ♡ K5
     ◇ 64
     ♣ 9763

     Bid 2♠

(b) ♠ AJ1074
     ♡ K5
     ◇ 64
     ♣ AJ97

     Bid 3♠

(c) ♠ AJ104
     ♡ KJ97
     ◇ 64
     ♣ AJ9

     Bid 3◇

(d) ♠ AJ104
     ♡ KJ97
     ◇ A10
     ♣ 973

     Bid 2NT
     then 3◇ over 3♣

(e) ♠ A74
     ♡ KJ7
     ◇ 64
     ♣ KQ1073

     Bid 3NT

(f) ♠ A74
     ♡ 75
     ◇ KJ4
     ♣ KQ1073

     Bid 2NT
     then 3NT over 3♣

(g) ♠ A74
     ♡ Q108
     ◇ K42
     ♣ Q1075

     Double

(h) ♠ 74
     ♡ K84
     ◇ 42
     ♣ KQ9753

     Bid 2NT

Bids in (a) and (b) are natural, (a) being competitive and non-forcing in the usual way, and (b) being forcing as in standard methods. (c) This is Stayman promising at least one four-card major without a stop in the opposition suit. (d) This requests partner to bid 3♣ and then, when South continues with 3◊, this becomes Stayman plus a stop in the enemy suit. In (e) this shows the values for 3NT without a stop. In (f) you are showing the values for game plus a stop. By doubling in (g) you show a natural raise to 2NT. (h) When partner bids 3♣, as requested, South passes.

North opens 1NT (12-14 points) and East overcalls with an artificial bid of 2♣ which shows the majors.

South holds:

(a)	♠ A1096	(b)	♠ 9	(c)	♠ K6
	♡ K6		♡ A63		♡ 10
	◊ A754		◊ KQ10742		◊ K10732
	♣ J62		♣ A75		♣ QJ974
	Double		Bid 3◊		Bid 2♡

(d)	♠ J4	(e)	♠ K6	(f)	♠ K6
	♡ 105		♡ 1053		♡ QJ5
	◊ AQJ53		◊ AQ75		◊ A10742
	♣ KQJ10		♣ KJ107		♣ K95
	Bid 2♠		Bid 3NT		Bid 2NT
					then 3NT over 3♣

(a) The double shows that South is willing to double at least one of the major suits for penalties. (b) This bid is forcing to game. (c) This is a non-game-going competitive bid with support for the unbid suits. (d) This shows values for game and support for the unbid suits. (e) Denies a stop in both majors but may have a stop in one of them. (f) Requests partner to bid 3♣, and then 3NT confirms a stop in both majors.

It is time to look at some complete deals:

Game All. Pairs. Dealer North.

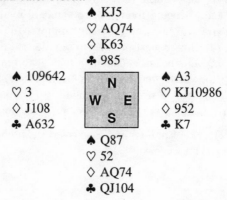

♠ KJ5
♥ AQ74
♦ K63
♣ 985

♠ 109642
♥ 3
♦ J108
♣ A632

♠ A3
♥ KJ10986
♦ 952
♣ K7

♠ Q87
♥ 52
♦ AQ74
♣ QJ104

At most tables North became the declarer in 2NT, just made after a heart lead. The popular bidding sequence was:

West	North	East	South
–	1NT	2♡	2NT
All Pass			

At one table where Lebensohl was employed by the North/South pair the bidding started the same way, 1NT–2♡, but then South doubled – showing the values to raise to 2NT. North happily passed, converting South's 'raise' into a penalty double. Neither the lead nor the defence made a lot of difference because there was no way declarer could avoid losing the obvious six tricks, three diamonds, one spade and two hearts. Plus 200 earned a barrelful of matchpoints.

Love All. IMPs. Dealer North.

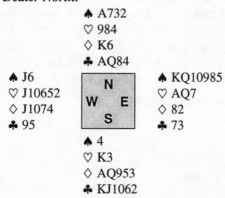

♠ A732
♥ 984
♦ K6
♣ AQ84

♠ J6
♥ J10652
♦ J1074
♣ 95

♠ KQ10985
♥ AQ7
♦ 82
♣ 73

♠ 4
♥ K3
♦ AQ953
♣ KJ1062

At one table this was the bidding:

West	North	East	South
–	1NT	2♠	3♠
Pass	3NT	All Pass	

The ♠K was led and North made just nine tricks for a score of 400.

At the opposite table North/South were playing Lebensohl:

West	North	East	South
–	1NT	2♠	3◇
Pass	3NT	Pass	4♣
Pass	4♠	Pass	6♣
All Pass			

As 3◇ was forcing South had plenty of time to show his suits. He reckoned that if North was unsuitable for a minor-suit contract he could always sign off in 4NT, which he (South) would pass. However, far from being unsuitable, North liked what he saw and signalled the good news with a cuebid in the enemy suit. Two long suits that fit together well invariably play for more tricks than the point count would seem to indicate, so South decided to take his chance in the slam. As it happened 6♣ was virtually ironclad, earning a score of 920 and a swing of 11 IMPs.

Lebensohl had played its part in achieving a fine score and there is little doubt that it is a useful gadget to have in your armoury. But it does tax the memory rather more than most bidding aids. You may have noticed!

Unassuming Cuebids

Star Rating: ✳✳✳

How closely can you define your values when your partner makes an overcall and you wish to support him? Suppose you are East and hold:

♠ K104
♡ A6
◇ 10653
♣ KJ93

The bidding starts like this:

West	North	East	South
–	–	–	1◇
1♠	Pass	?	

You have quite a respectable hand, with handsome support for spades, but how can this information be conveyed to partner without, on the one hand going too high, while, on the other, failing to impress him sufficiently, with the result that game is missed? Perhaps you decide on a value bid of 3♠ only to find that this is the full hand:

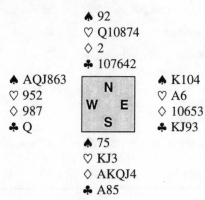

                    ♠ 92
                    ♡ Q10874
                    ◇ 2
                    ♣ 107642

    ♠ AQJ863   ♠ K104
    ♡ 952   ♡ A6
    ◇ 987   ◇ 10653
    ♣ Q   ♣ KJ93

                    ♠ 75
                    ♡ KJ3
                    ◇ AKQJ4
                    ♣ A85

Unfortunately eight tricks in spades is your limit, and, to make matters worse, North/South can't make any contract above the two level. So, perhaps you should have bid only 2♠ – but then, if we rearrange the West hand slightly, giving it just two more points, the ♣A instead of the ♣Q and the ♣7 instead of the ◇7, would West not be sorely tempted to pass 2♠? Pity, because now ten tricks are icy. However, worry not because help is at hand with the Unassuming Cuebid, a device that is employed to contend with these very problems.

In the old traditional way, a cuebid in the opposition suit was game-forcing, showing not only a powerful hand but, in all probability, strong support for partner's suit. When you play Unassuming Cuebids you do not forgo this feature – you adopt another as well. The new feature, which takes priority initially, denotes sound support for partner, as opposed to mainly distributional values. About 11+, or perhaps a good 10, are the minimum points associated with an Unassuming Cuebid. The corollary is that direct raises, to whatever level, are based on distributional, rather than high-card strength.

I am indebted to my cruise colleague, Gus Calderwood, for a further idea that helps to streamline your responses. After partner's overcall you respond 2NT:

           1◇   1♠   Pass   2NT

that is fairly normal showing about 12-13 points, but when you precede your 2NT bid with an Unassuming Cuebid:

1♢	1♠	Pass	2♢
Pass	2♠	Pass	2NT

you should then show 14-15 points. Let's look at some examples:

South opens 1♢, West bids 1♠, North passes and East holds:

> **(a)** ♠ QJ9
> ♡ J64
> ♢ 106
> ♣ KJ853

Raise to 2♠. You are not good enough for an Unassuming Cuebid.

> **(b)** ♠ K1074
> ♡ J6
> ♢ 94
> ♣ KQ764

Raise to 3♠. With mainly distributional values, a limit raise is best.

> **(c)** ♠ QJ9
> ♡ KQ8
> ♢ 74
> ♣ A10864

Bid 2♢. With good top cards and sound support in partner's suit you start with an Unassuming Cuebid which is forcing to agreement.

> **(d)** ♠ AQ84
> ♡ A5
> ♢ 743
> ♣ AK109

Bid 2♢. Again an Unassuming Cuebid but this time you will not let the bidding stop short of game.

> **(e)** ♠ 1063
> ♡ AJ9
> ♢ KJ6
> ♣ KJ109

Bid 2NT. A fairly normal response indicating 12-13 points and a balanced hand with either a doubleton or three small spades.

(f) ♠ 1063
♡ AQ97
◇ KQ10
♣ KJ9

Bid 2◇. You start with an Unassuming Cuebid and intend to follow it with 2NT showing 14-15 points.

Perhaps the third player makes a low-level bid. That need not disrupt your responses.

South opens 1◇, West bids 1♡, North 1♠ and East holds:

(a) ♠ A1043
♡ KJ5
◇ J6
♣ QJ95

Bid 2◇. With so much bidding going on, it is quite likely that a part-score will be your limit, but you have the right values for an Unassuming Cuebid so you should certainly make it.

(b) ♠ 104
♡ Q853
◇ A1054
♣ 863

Raise to 2♡. At favourable vulnerability it might be tempting to increase the ante by bidding 3♡, but partner would expect a little more, say ...

(c) ♠ 10
♡ K853
◇ A1054
♣ J1084

Raise to 3♡.

(d) ♠ K1043
♡ J6
◇ AK5
♣ Q1064

Bid 2NT. This describes your hand well, both in points and distribution.

(e) ♠ KJ73
     ♡ J6
     ◇ AK5
     ♣ Q1097

Bid 2◇. If West continues with 2♡, rebid 2NT showing the balanced nature of your hand plus the point count (14-15).

Overcaller's Reaction to the Unassuming Cuebid

(a) With a minimum hand, overcaller rebids his suit at the lowest level.

(b) With additional values, he makes a jump bid in his suit or bids a second suit.

(c) With game-going values, he bids game or cuebid opponent's suit.

South opens 1♣, West bids 1♠, North passes, East bids 2♣, what do you do as West holding:

(a) ♠ AQ10864
     ♡ 753
     ◇ J97
     ♣ 4

Rebid 2♠. You are minimum and have no ambitions beyond a partscore.

(b) ♠ AK1086
     ♡ KJ4
     ◇ Q10
     ♣ 863

Rebid 3♠. With one more heart and one less club you would rebid 2♡.

(c) ♠ AQ10974
     ♡ K7
     ◇ QJ107
     ♣ 7

Rebid 4♠. There should be few problems.

(d) ♠ KJ7543
     ♡ KQ
     ◇ 75
     ♣ A74

Rebid 3♣. With the right cards in partner's hand a slam is a possibility.

Here is a hand that occurred in a local club duplicate.

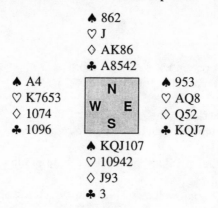

♠ 862
♡ J
◇ AK86
♣ A8542

♠ A4
♡ K7653
◇ 1074
♣ 1096

♠ 953
♡ AQ8
◇ Q52
♣ KQJ7

♠ KQJ107
♡ 10942
◇ J93
♣ 3

The bidding might make purists wince but these things happen:

West	North	East	South
–	–	1♣	1♠
2♡	3♡	Double	3♠
All Pass			

The ♠A and another spade would have defeated the contract but, not unreasonably, West led the ♣10. Declarer won in dummy and played a heart to East's ♡A. Now the ♠A and a second spade cut down dummy's ruffing power, but declarer was still able to obtain one heart ruff and then exit with a low diamond. East went in with the ◇Q, and cashed the ♡Q, but that was the end of the defence. 3♠ just made. Note how North, with an Unassuming Cuebid, was able to get his values over to partner without rocking the boat.

The Unassuming Cuebid paves the way for an exchange of information at a relatively low level. This can be invaluable in competitive auctions.

Protection

Star Rating: ✷✷✷✷✷

Protection is certainly no racket! It is a most important ingredient of good bridge and unless you are tactically well equipped in this department you will be unable to cope effectively with many everyday situations. The Americans call it Balancing, which has always struck me as a more appropriate term, but whatever the name – Protection or Balancing – the aims are the same.

The purpose of a Protective Bid

When the opposition are about to buy at a low level, partner having passed, for example:

West	North	East	South
1◇	Pass	Pass	?

or

West	North	East	South
–	–	1♡	Pass
2♡	Pass	Pass	?

it is often in one's interests to contest the auction, sometimes on quite modest values. The idea is either to buy for your own side or to push the opponents over the top.

Why is it necessary to protect?

If the bidding is about to die at a low level in the opposition's best suit/fit, it is not unusual for your partner to have some fair values, although he has not so far felt able to bid. When you now enter the fray you are protecting his pass, or, as they say on the other side of the Atlantic, you are Balancing. This duty absolves partner from entering the auction on unsuitable hands when his side may be totally outgunned.

Before we start to define our various bids in the protective position let us make quite sure what it is we expect from our partner, prior to being faced with a Protection or Balancing problem.

1. We expect partner to make an overcall on a respectable suit – length and quality of suit being more important than a high number of points. Of course, the vulnerability and the level at which partner can enter the auction are very relevant.

2. We expect partner to use an informatory (take-out) double on suitable hands that have adequate support for unbid suits, especially unbid majors.

3. We expect partner to overcall 1NT on a strong balanced hand; with about 16-18 points and the suit bid well held.

4. We expect partner to take appropriate action on strongly distributional hands that call for a systemic bid (Unusual no-trumps, pre-empts, Michaels Cuebid etc).

So it seems that our partner's biggest 'problem' will be on hands where he would have opened the bidding comfortably enough, but because the opposition have got there first, he is left without a sensible bid to make. In fact, this is not really a problem at all, as it is almost always right to pass and rely on partner to protect, if that seems the right thing for him to do.

Suppose RHO opens 1♡ and you hold:

(a)	♠ A4	(b)	♠ 86	(c)	♠ Q654	(d)	♠ J3
	♡ KJ73		♡ AJ964		♡ KJ92		♡ Q74
	◊ K1062		◊ KQ52		◊ 7		◊ AQ86
	♣ Q82		♣ A6		♣ AQJ5		♣ KQ54

You should, of course, pass in each case. Indeed, pass has so much going for it that any alternative action can hardly be regarded as a serious contender.

If there are still any doubts about passing on modest balanced hands after RHO has opened the bidding, let us consider three common situations. East opens one of a suit on 13 points, South passes on 13 balanced points. This leaves 14 points at large.

Case 1: West holds all, or nearly all, the missing points, so North is marked with a worthless hand. East/West bid to game and would no doubt have done so whether South had spoken or not. The difference is that South has given nothing away and furthermore did not offer the opposition the chance of a juicy double, should they have preferred that option. In defence South knows more or less what to expect from his partner. East/West must proceed in the dark.

Conclusion: South was right not to interfere.

Case 2: North holds all, or nearly all, the missing points, thus when West has to pass his partner's opening bid North enters the auction. Now there is nothing to stop North/South arriving in their optimum contract.

Conclusion: South has lost nothing by passing in second position.

Case 3: The missing 14 points are approximately equally shared between the West and North players. It is now anyone's guess as to which side can make a contract. Quite often whoever plays it goes down, but in any case the bidding is likely to stop at a low level, which will give North/South another chance to assess their prospects.

Conclusion: a grey area, but no serious disadvantage occasioned by South's pass.

The overall conclusion therefore is that the second player, South in my examples, stands to lose little and gain a lot by passing on moderate balanced hands when RHO opens the bidding. This brings us to the fourth player, North, who is in the protective position.

Action to be taken by the player in the Protective Position

West	North	East	South
–	–	1◊	Pass
Pass	?		

1. Bid 2NT on a strong balanced hand, 19-21 points (some play 20-22).

2. Bid 1NT on a weak balanced hand, 11-13 points. Popular ranges vary here, but perhaps it is easy to remember that your 3 point range starts at 1 point less than your 1NT opening (12-14), which, incidentally, is in line with your protection bid of 2NT which also starts at 1 point less that your normal opening bid of 2NT (20-22).

3. Make a jump bid in a suit with a sound opening bid and a six card suit.

4. Bid a respectable suit if you have 10-12 points.

5. Bid two of opponent's suit on strong two-suiters.

6. Double on all other strong hands not necessarily ideal in shape, but too powerful to approach in any other way. Also double on ideal shapely hands with about 11+ points.

You are North in the following examples. The bidding proceeds:

West	North	East	South
–	–	1♡	Pass
Pass	?		

(a) ♠ AQ10
     ♡ KJ6
     ◊ K1094
     ♣ AQJ

     Bid 2NT

(b) ♠ A6
     ♡ QJ106
     ◊ A1075
     ♣ 1074

     Bid 1NT

(c) ♠ A1063
     ♡ K63
     ◊ KQ10
     ♣ AJ9

Double, then consider bidding 2NT over partner's two of a minor.

(d) ♠ A6
     ♡ 863
     ◇ AJ75
     ♣ K954

Bid 1NT. Don't let the three small hearts worry you. The missing honours are even better placed when they are in partner's hand.

(e) ♠ AKJ96   (f) ♠ AKJ986   (g) ♠ KQ9875
     ♡ 863   ♡ 63   ♡ 8
     ◇ QJ9   ◇ QJ9   ◇ –
     ♣ 53   ♣ K3   ♣ AKJ1086

     Bid 1♠   Bid 2♠   Bid 2♡

*(h)♠ K6   *(i) ♠ AQ6   *(j) ♠ K863   *(k) ♠ Q
    ♡ AQ10   ♡ 86   ♡ 6   ♡ A85
    ◇ KQ95   ◇ AKJ95   ◇ AK95   ◇ AQJ105
    ♣ J1065   ♣ 1096   ♣ J1094   ♣ KQ108

* Double in each case. A protective double covers a wide range of hands.

As with the use of most conventional gadgets, common sense should always prevail in questionable circumstances. For example, at love all West opens 1♣ which is passed to you in the South seat. You hold:

                    ♠ 6
                    ♡ A64
                    ◇ KQ83
                    ♣ KJ1097

You have the values to protect, but wait a minute. Where have all the spades gone? Your partner did not overcall, so they have probably got a fit. If you disturb one club you may find yourself trying to defend 4♠. This is no time for heroics – pass.

This hand occurred in a teams event. You might like to consider the problem from the West position. This is what you hold as West at game to your side, dealer South:

                    ♠ J1076
                    ♡ Q
                    ◇ KJ103
                    ♣ K1092

South opens 1♡, you pass, North raises to 2♡, East passes and South, after giving it a little thought, also passes. It is now up to you .... I can hear you saying, 'Well, what do you want from my life? Of course I pass.'

No doubt you are right but this is a tight match. You are fighting for every point and every point is vital so, against your better judgement perhaps, you double. North quickly raises to 3♡, East passes and South now bids 4♡. Everyone passes and with a sinking feeling that on this occasion your judgement, at best, is questionable and at worst certifiable, you lead the ♠J. The sight of dummy does nothing to restore your faith in the righteous! This is what you see:

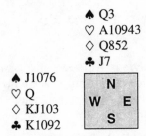

                    ♠ Q3
                    ♡ A10943
                    ◊ Q852
                    ♣ J7

♠ J1076
♡ Q
◊ KJ103
♣ K1092

'What was that *two*-heart bid?' you mutter to yourself. 'He must have thought he was playing with his grandmother. Surely anyone with red blood in his veins bids 3♡.'

The ♠J is covered by dummy's ♠Q, partner's ♠K and declarer's ♠A. Trumps are drawn in two rounds ending in dummy, and then the ♠3 is led. Partner plays the ♠8, declarer the ♠9 and you win with the ♠10. How do you continue? In fact, partner, bless him, has told you. This was the full hand:

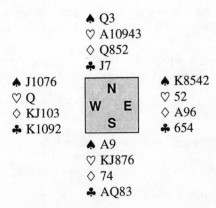

                    ♠ Q3
                    ♡ A10943
                    ◊ Q852
                    ♣ J7

♠ J1076   ♠ K8542
♡ Q   ♡ 52
◊ KJ103   ◊ A96
♣ K1092   ♣ 654

                    ♠ A9
                    ♡ KJ876
                    ◊ 74
                    ♣ AQ83

That ♠8 was a most thoughtful play – a McKenney suit preference signal asking for a diamond, not a club. A club switch sees declarer home. A diamond switch and the contract has to go one down.

Seldom has plus 50 looked so handsome on the scoresheet. Faith is restored in almost everything and balancing is even more firmly established in the bidding repertoire. Of course, if you don't want to live quite so dangerously as this last example would seem to suggest, there are still plenty of opportunities for Protection/Balancing which are of a less flamboyant, more mundane nature. They, too, can be both profitable and enjoyable.

Michaels Cuebid

Star Rating: ✳✳

My early experiences of playing with team-mates who were using Michaels Cuebids were memorable, if not exactly favourable. Going through the score card there would be a pregnant pause over a figure of, say, minus 800 and then later on minus 1100.

'What happened there?' we would ask. The reply began to have a familiar ring about it. 'Ah, well you see that was a Michaels Cuebid.'

I like to think we nodded gravely, smiled sympathetically and continued discreetly to the next hand, but of course it is always possible that my memory is somewhat clouded with the passing of time!

That may not sound like a very auspicious start for a gadget that Eric Crowhurst tells us is now officially part of Acol in the '90s but – to use a motoring term as an analogy – it's not really the car that kills, it's the driver. However, it must be admitted that a Michaels Cuebid is a highly explosive and volatile gadget, so it is essential to use it with care.

The basic structure of Michaels Cuebid
By cuebidding the opponent's suit directly, you show a two-suited hand as follows:

1♣   2♣   or   1◇   2◇

Shows at least 5-4, preferably 5-5 in the major suits.

1♡   2♡   or   1♠   2♠

Shows at least five of the unbid major and a five card or longer minor suit.

The sixty-four thousand dollar question is, 'How strong should the cue-bidder be?' It is certainly advisable for regular partnerships to discuss this point, although I observe that Eric Crowhurst's findings suggest a Michaels Cuebid should be 'weak, pre-emptive and shapely'. This would seem to leave an uncomfortable void for the stronger hands, but if the mood of the '90s dictates a weak, pre-emptive version, then so be it.

Obviously, vulnerability will play a vital part in deciding the partnership action and, while there is considerable scope for obstructive interference at favourable vulnerability, one would require a more freakish distribution, or a stronger version, before taking action at unfavourable vulnerability.

You will notice that, over one of a minor, a Michaels Cuebid can be made when 5-4 in the majors, although 5-5 is certainly preferable. If you are only 5-4, then it is advisable to ensure there is some substance in these suits, especially in the four-card suit. For example:

♠ AQ108
♡ KQ1087
♢ 8
♣ 1074

would be acceptable, but:

♠ Q754
♡ KJ543
♢ 8
♣ KJ4

would be decidedly risky.

I am loath to prescribe a minimum point count because distribution, intermediate and working cards, together with vulnerability, play such an important part. However, I suppose 6 or 7 points would be acceptable if all other factors are in your favour, otherwise 8-12 points would be normal in the weak pre-emptive version. Let us look at some examples:

Not vulnerable *versus* vulnerable: East opens 1♡, South holds:

♠ AJ1096
♡ 4
♢ 63
♣ Q10985

Bid 2♡. You have the equipment.

East opens 1♡, South holds, vulnerable *versus* not vulnerable:

♠ AJ1096
♡ 4
◊ 6
♣ QJ10986

Bid 2♡. Despite adverse conditions and a comparatively low point count, the shape and intermediates are such that only the faint-hearted would miss this opportunity.

East opens 1♡, South holds at equal vulnerability:

♠ KQ1074
♡ 43
◊ AJ1076
♣ 3

Bid 2♡. This would be a fairly normal hand for unleashing your missile.

East opens 1♡, South holds at any vulnerability:

♠ Q9654
♡ 43
◊ 6
♣ KJ643

Pass. A good pass at any vulnerability.

It is always tempting to play around with a new toy but, if you are going to avoid those pregnant pauses as you announce minus 800 or minus 1100, it is wise to keep your Michaels Cuebid up to strength commensurate with the vulnerability. In its weak form, a Michaels Cuebid is an obstructive weapon, so clearly some risks are justified, just as they are with all pre-emptive bids. But unless you enjoy living dangerously, it is sensible to consider the risk of a misfit. If you open the bidding with 3♡ on:

♠ 4
♡ KQJ10976
◊ J106
♣ 84

you can be fairly sure you will take six tricks, misfit or not, so your liability can be measured.

If you overcall 1♠ with 2♠ on:

♠ 4
♡ KQ975
◇ A9743
♣ 86

you are entering an unknown area. Your liabilities will very much depend
on partner's shape and high cards. If he is with you in one of the red suits
then no doubt you have done the right thing, but if he is short in the red
suits you may be in for an uncomfortable ride, eventually conceding a
sizeable penalty, possibly in a doubtful cause. Such are the hazards of
Michaels Cuebids.

I think I have now issued enough warnings, so let's look on the positive
side. There is plenty going for us, and on a good day even miracles can happen. Remember also, despite my misgivings, the majority of experts give
this conventional gadget the thumbs up and they would not do so unless
they were reasonably confident of an overall gain. So our thanks to the late
Mr M Michaels of Miami Beach for an interesting and provocative convention which has at last found official favour with the British bridge elite.

Before we go on to look at some hands we ought to analyse partner's reaction to our Michaels Cuebid.

Partner's reaction to our Michaels Cuebid
1. He should bid the full value of his hand if there is a known fit, sometimes making an advance sacrifice to pressurise the opponents.

2. If he cannot support the major he can bid 2NT to ask his partner to
name his minor suit. If 2NT is not available because of opposition bidding, then a cuebid in the opponent's suit will serve the same purpose.

At game all West opens 1◇, North bids 2◇ and East passes, South holds:

(a)   ♠ KJ95
      ♡ A10
      ◇ 764
      ♣ AKJ10

Bid 3◇. You are rather too good to shut up shop with 4♠. If North holds
a singleton diamond a slam is a live possibility.

(b) ♠ K9754
♡ A10
◊ 7643
♣ J4

Bid 4♠. You may or may not succeed but tactically this bid is sound enough.

(c) ♠ 75
♡ K84
◊ J1096
♣ Q1084

Bid 2♡. There is no other choice. Since both suits are known 2NT would be natural, but this is not the hand for that bid.

At game all West opens 1♡, North bids 2♡ and East passes.

(d) ♠ 75
♡ A863
◊ Q9
♣ J9742

Bid 2NT. If partner's second suit is clubs you may have a good sacrifice, if it is diamonds you should pass 3◊.

(e) ♠ QJ75
♡ J863
◊ AK7
♣ 42

Bid 3♠. The full value of the hand in the known fit.

With East/West vulnerable, West opens 1♠, North bids 2♠ and East raises to 3♠. South holds:

(f) ♠ 82
♡ 5
◊ Q10864
♣ KQ973

Bid 4♠. You want to know partner's minor suit. Maybe there is a cheap save available.

This hand featured some ambitious bidding which was rewarded by a slight slip in defence.

Game All. Dealer North.

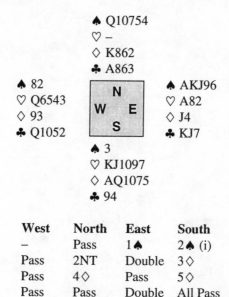

```
                    ♠ Q10754
                    ♡ –
                    ◇ K862
                    ♣ A863
    ♠ 82                         ♠ AKJ96
    ♡ Q6543        N             ♡ A82
    ◇ 93         W   E           ◇ J4
    ♣ Q1052        S             ♣ KJ7
                    ♠ 3
                    ♡ KJ1097
                    ◇ AQ1075
                    ♣ 94
```

West	North	East	South
–	Pass	1♠	2♠ (i)
Pass	2NT	Double	3◇
Pass	4◇	Pass	5◇
Pass	Pass	Double	All Pass

(i) Michaels Cuebid

Despite the fact that East/West have slightly more in high cards than North/South, it is the latter who have the all-important fit, nicely located by a Michaels Cuebid. Clearly, 5◇ was going to be no pushover and the really critical point arrived at trick two. The ♠8 was led, covered by the ♠10 and ♠J, and now the spotlight fell on East. Had he switched to a club – and there is certainly a strong case for this – the contract would have failed. In fact he tried to cash the ♠A. Declarer ruffed and ran the ♡9 to East's ♡A, discarding a club from dummy when West played low. Now the club switch was won by the ♣A and two rounds of trumps gave South the lead to continue hearts. A second club was discarded on the ♡K, the ♡Q was ruffed out and dummy's last club disappeared on declarer's last heart. The rest of the tricks were made on a cross-ruff. Contract just made.

So Michaels Cuebid performed really well, albeit with a little luck in running.

My last hand illustrates the now familiar theme that shape is so very much more important than points.

North/South Game. Pairs. Dealer North.

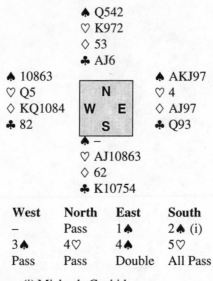

```
                    ♠ Q542
                    ♡ K972
                    ◊ 53
                    ♣ AJ6
     ♠ 10863                        ♠ AKJ97
     ♡ Q5          ┌─────────┐      ♡ 4
     ◊ KQ1084      │    N    │      ◊ AJ97
     ♣ 82          │  W   E  │      ♣ Q93
                   │    S    │
                   └─────────┘
                    ♠ –
                    ♡ AJ10863
                    ◊ 62
                    ♣ K10754
```

West	North	East	South
–	Pass	1♠	2♠ (i)
3♠	4♡	4♠	5♡
Pass	Pass	Double	All Pass

(i) Michaels Cuebid

East's double looks very ill-judged. He would have done much better to follow the policy of bidding one for the road – or would he? It is OK if East/West buy, then 5♠ will go quietly one down, but what happens if North/South also bid one for the road and continue to 6♡? On this sequence East would surely cash his ◊ A and with the South hand on the table the defence can hardly go wrong, but you never know....

Against 5♡ doubled, East led his ♠A and declarer saw at once that locating the ♣Q was going to be worth a million dollars. It was fair to presume that the ◊ A and ◊ K were split (with both honours East would surely have led a diamond) but of course it was impossible to get even an approximate count of the hand. Certainly, East was short in hearts, but then he probably had more spades than West. Perhaps the deciding factor for North was East's aggressive bidding, so, having ruffed the spade and drawn trumps, he played the ♣A and ♣J. East ducked smoothly, but declarer had made up his mind and let the ♣J run. A few seconds later he collected all thirteen tricks.

This time Michaels Cuebid played a rather less dynamic role in the bidding because most Souths would come in with their heart suit over 1♠. Nevertheless, it was the second suit which did so much damage and that, of course, is a key feature of the Michaels Cuebid.

I would like to conclude by giving a brief summary of the pros and cons of using the Michaels Cuebid.

For

Even used with care this is not a gadget to be tucked away in the cupboard and just trotted out on special occasions. It is an everyday weapon, obstructive, pre-emptive and at moments quite devastating. It provokes action, creates swings and, used in conjunction with the Unusual 2NT (this shows length in the two lowest-ranking unbid suits), makes you well-equipped to compete. With a little help from the opposition, almost unbelievable results are achieved.

Against

As with all bids showing weak distributional hands, a great deal of information passes into enemy hands. This does not enhance your defensive prospects when they buy the contract. With a misfit, the Michaels missile can behave like a boomerang and come zooming back to the sender with unpleasant consequences. 800s and 1100s come suddenly to mind. Then, having given over the immediate cuebid of the enemy suit to weak pre-emptive hands, strong two-suiters:

♠ AQJ974
♡ –
◇ KQJ106
♣ AQ

and exceptionally powerful one-suited hands are difficult to bid with any degree of accuracy. No doubt one has to fall back on the informatory double, but that is an improvisation which clearly has defects. Of course, the pro Michaels Cuebid fans would argue that these very strong hands occur only once in a blue moon. No doubt that is right but they are certainly difficult to bid without proper equipment when that blue moon emerges.

Let's hope your misfits are travelling companions of the blue moon!

Multi Two Diamonds

Star rating: ✳✳✳

One of the most useful conventions to arrive on the bridge scene in comparatively modern times must surely be the 'Multi'. Brainchild of the late Jeremy Flint and expounded in depth in a number of publications by that doyen of all British writers, Terence Reese, the Multi has captured the imagination of players all over the world. Hardly surprising perhaps, when one considers the scope enjoyed by this gadget, embracing as it does weak hands, strong hands and almost unbiddable hands.

Although there are a number of versions of the Multi in circulation I plan to give you a balanced, sensible and eminently playable method since this is no place to discuss the more eccentric or complex off-shoots that invariably cloud the horizon, whenever a new weapon enters the bridge armoury.

The opening bid of 2◇ covers three distinctly different types of hand:

    (i) A weak two in either major, 6-10 points.
    (ii) A strong two in either minor: Acol, 8-9 playing tricks.
    (iii) A balanced hand of 23-24 points.

To reminisce for a moment. If only Skid Simon were alive today how delighted he would be to see that the weak two can be used while still retaining his beloved Acol two (Skid, in conjunction with Jack Marx, invented the Acol Two bid). In his classic book, *Design for Bidding*, Simon made it a close choice between opting for weak twos or Acol twos (note it had to be a choice), finally giving the nod to what he admitted might be a prejudiced vote in favour of largely his own creation. Now, some forty years on, we can enjoy all the advantages of a weak two opening while our initial bid of 2♠ or 2♡ is still pure Acol. Let us look at some typical hands in each category.

(i) A Weak Two in either major:

(a) ♠ KQ10864	**(b)** ♠ 32	**(c)** ♠ 2
♡ 6	♡ AQJ975	♡ KQJ1084
◇ K96	◇ 10987	◇ 832
♣ 742	♣ 6	♣ KJ7

The opening bid in each case is 2◇. At the first opportunity opener will indicate a weak two in his long suit. A respectable six-card is the hallmark of this gambit.

(ii) A Strong Two in either minor (Acol, 8-9 playing tricks):

(a) ♠ 3	**(b)** ♠ A107	**(c)** ♠ 4
♡ A74	♡ A	♡ AK
◊ AKQJ95	◊ KQ9	◊ A32
♣ AJ6	♣ AQJ1074	♣ KQJ10974

The opening bid in each case is 2◊. As soon as possible opener will indicate that this time he has a hand of power and quality with 8-9 playing tricks, with hand (a) he will rebid diamonds and with (b) and (c) clubs.

You will notice one important development here. In traditional (old-fashioned?) Acol there is no way to show a powerful hand with 8-9 playing tricks when the main suit is clubs. You simply have to improvise, but when you play the Multi this problem is overcome.

(iii) A Balanced hand of 23-24 points:

(a) ♠ AK10	**(b)** ♠ A63	**(c)** ♠ AKJ
♡ KQJ	♡ Q1094	♡ AQ8
◊ AJ95	◊ AKJ	◊ K64
♣ KQJ	♣ AKQ	♣ AQ1065

As before, the opening bid in each case is 2◊. But now opener intends to rebid no trumps at the first opportunity which will inform his partner that he has a hand of this nature.

Although the 23-24 point count for the strong balanced version of the Multi is not universally played, I strongly advise it because it creates an important advantage in another area. In traditional Acol the sequence 2♣–2◊–2NT is non-forcing because opener is showing 23-24 points and if partner has nothing, or almost nothing, there is no virtue in stretching for an improbable game. Thus if opener has 25+ he has to rebid 3NT himself (2♣–2◊–3NT). But if your balanced version of the Multi shows 23-24 points (you open 2◊ and rebid 2NT) it follows that the sequence 2♣–2◊–2NT must be forcing as it now shows 25+. This development is an obvious advantage as you have more bidding space and it is no longer incumbent on you to jump about like a kangaroo with the bare minimum point count necessary for game.

Responder's initial reaction to opener's Multi 2◊

Responder should always assume, until advised otherwise, that opener has a weak two in one of the majors. On this basis, if he is content to play in a low-level contract he responds as follows:

2♡ – if opener has a weak two in hearts he will pass.

2♠ – if opener has a weak two in spades he will pass, but if his suit is
hearts he will bid 3♡ with a minimum and 4♡ with a maximum.

When responder is strong and wishes to discover his partner's type of
hand he bids 2NT – a forcing relay.

Any response at the three level is natural and forcing.

The most likely bid for responder to make is 2♡ (2◊–2♡) which covers all
weak hands and would be the equivalent of passing a weak 2♡ opening.

Perhaps the response of 2♠ (2◊–2♠) may sound slightly strange because
in fact it shows support for *hearts*. Of course, if opener has a weak two in
spades he passes and, as already indicated, with a weak two in hearts he
rebids his suit at the three or four level depending on strength.

Opener's rebid when responder enquires with 2NT (2◊–2NT)
With a weak two in the majors, he rebids like this:

3♡ – lower range weak two in hearts.
3♠ – lower range weak two in spades.
3♣ – upper range weak two in hearts.
3◊ – upper range weak two in spades.

With a 23-24 point balanced hand he rebids 3NT.

With an Acol two in clubs or diamonds he must rebid four of his minor.

Opener's Rebid on strong hands when Responder bids 2♡ (2◊–2♡)
With an Acol two in clubs or diamonds he rebids three of his minor. With
a worthless hand responder can then pass.

With a 23-24 point balanced hand he rebids 2NT. Again, with a worthless
hand responder can pass.

Let's look at some examples.

The bidding starts: West 2◊–East 2♡. West holds:

(a)   ♠ AQJ976
       ♡ 6
       ◊ 10875
       ♣ 42

Rebid 2♠ showing a weak two in spades. Interchange the major suits and
you would then pass 2♡.

(b) ♠ AQ108
♡ KJ9
◊ AKJ
♣ AJ10

Rebid 2NT showing a balanced 23-24 points.

(c) ♠ AJ
♡ 6
◊ AKQJ97
♣ A652

Rebid 3◊ showing a typical Acol 2◊ opening with 8-9 playing tricks. Interchange the minor suits and you would rebid 3♣.

The bidding starts: West 2◊–East 2♠. West holds:

(a) ♠ AKJ976
♡ 6
◊ 753
♣ 542

Pass. Partner is not interested in playing higher than 2♠.

(b) ♠ K4
♡ QJ10964
◊ 1053
♣ 82

Rebid 3♡. You are in the lower range.

(c) ♠ A4
♡ KQ10964
◊ 753
♣ 82

Rebid 4♡. You are now in the upper range.

The bidding starts: West 2◊ – East 2NT. West holds:

(a) ♠ KJ10875
♡ 42
◊ QJ7
♣ 86

Rebid 3♠. You have a weak two in the lower range.

(b) ♠ AQJ1087
♡ 42
◇ QJ4
♣ 64

Rebid 3◇ showing a weak two in spades in the upper range.

(c) ♠ 6
♡ QJ9865
◇ A32
♣ 864

Rebid 3♡. You have a weak two in the lower range.

(d) ♠ 6
♡ AKJ963
◇ J1075
♣ 42

Rebid 3♣ showing a weak two in hearts in the upper range.

(e) ♠ KJ7
♡ AQJ
◇ AKJ7
♣ A64

Rebid 3NT showing 23-24 balanced points.

(f) ♠ 6
♡ Q108
◇ AKQJ74
♣ AK10

Rebid 4◇ showing an Acol two in diamonds. Interchange the minor suits and you would rebid 4♣ showing a similar hand with clubs.

The bidding starts: West 2◇ – East 3♣/3◇/3♡/3♠

1. ♠ 743
♡ AQJ1074
◇ J10
♣ 52

	N	
W		E
	S	

♠ AQ
♡ 6
◇ AKQ862
♣ KJ109

West	East
2◇	3◇
3♡	3NT
Pass	

When East discovers that West has a weak two in hearts – as expected – he subsides in 3NT.

2. ♠ 2
   ♡ AK10964
   ◇ 10964
   ♣ 62

		N		
W				E
		S		

   ♠ AQJ95
   ♡ 7
   ◇ KQJ
   ♣ KQJ10

West	East
2◇	3♠
3NT(i)	Pass

(i) West must have a
    weak two in hearts.

3. ♠ KQ10974
   ♡ J97
   ◇ K4
   ♣ 84

		N		
W				E
		S		

   ♠ AJ6
   ♡ Q
   ◇ A6
   ♣ AKJ10962

West	East
2◇	3♣
3♠	4NT
5♣	6♠
Pass	

East was pleasantly surprised to hear West's rebid and immediately set course for slam. West denied an ace but East was quite happy with 6♠ – an easy make.

One don't
Don't open 2◇ with a weak two, when you have four cards in the other major, for example:

                    ♠ A1096
                    ♡ KJ10974
                    ◇ 7
                    ♣ 32

It is best to pass and await developments. The danger of employing the Multi is that you might play in 2♡ with 4♠ laydown.

Here is an exciting hands involving the Multi, which was played in a head-to-head teams match.

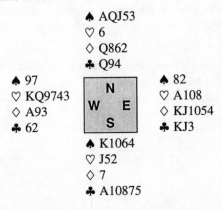

                    ♠ AQJ53
                    ♡ 6
                    ◇ Q862
                    ♣ Q94

   ♠ 97
   ♡ KQ9743
   ◇ A93
   ♣ 62

   ♠ 82
   ♡ A108
   ◇ KJ1054
   ♣ KJ3

                    ♠ K1064
                    ♡ J52
                    ◇ 7
                    ♣ A10875

In Room 1 this was the bidding:

West	North	East	South
–	–	–	Pass
Pass	1♠	2◇	4♠
All Pass			

South was a player not renowned for underbidding so his jump to game was fairly typical. In any case, it is hard to grumble with success as, rightly or wrongly, West was silenced. A diamond and a heart were taken by the defence and the second heart was ruffed. Trumps were drawn in two rounds and then the ♣Q found the ♣K at home. So declarer lost three tricks: one heart, one diamond and one club.

In Room 2 the bidding took a very different course:

West	North	East	South
–	–	–	Pass
2◇	Pass	2♠	Pass
4♡	All Pass		

2◇ was the Multi and 2♠ showed willingness to play there if that was partner's suit. At the same time East's bid showed heart support and left partner to say whether he was maximum or minimum, if indeed he had a weak two in hearts. West was maximum, so he duly bid game.

With very little to guide him North's lead was something of a guess. In fact if West plays the minor suits to advantage ten tricks will roll in no matter what the defence scheme up. In practice, West was not severely tested when the ◇2 hit the table. Trumps were drawn and the run of the diamond suit provided eleven tricks, declarer ditching two spades. Then a right guess in clubs brought the total to twelve. Plus 620 in one room and plus 680 in the other gave one of the teams a swing of 16 IMPs – a result you dream about.

The Multi is something I can recommend with considerable confidence. It is fun to play and it has its moments!